When You Listen to This Song

When You Listen to This Song

On Memory, Loss, and Writing

LOLA LAFON

Translated by Lauren Elkin

Yale
UNIVERSITY PRESS
NEW HAVEN & LONDON

This work received support for excellence in publication and translation from Albertine Translation, a program created by Villa Albertine and funded by **Albertine Foundation.**

Yale University Press books may be purchased in quantity for educational, business, or promotional use. For information, please email sales.press@yale.edu (U.S. office) or sales@yaleup.co.uk (U.K. office).

Set in Spectral type by IDS Infotech Ltd.
Printed in the United States of America.

Library of Congress Control Number: 2025939551
ISBN 978-0-300-27588-9 (hardcover)

A catalogue record for this book is available from the British Library.

Authorized Representative in the EU: Easy Access System Europe, Mustamäe tee 50, 10621 Tallinn, Estonia, gpsr.requests@easproject.com

10 9 8 7 6 5 4 3 2 1

Men are accomplices to that which leaves them indifferent.
—George Steiner

Look at things which, though absent, are yet present firmly to thought.
—Parmenides

CONTENTS

WHEN YOU LISTEN TO THIS SONG 1

ACKNOWLEDGMENTS 161

TRANSLATOR'S NOTE 163

When You Listen to This Song

It's her. A silhouette at the window, emerging from the shadows, just a girl. She leans over the ledge, drawn, no doubt, by laughter she's heard in the street: it's coming from an elegant procession of people in satin gowns and gray suits.

She turns around, seems to be calling to someone. A wedding! Come and see! Impatiently she summons them again. Come quick! It's all so beautiful—the gleaming fabric, the lustrous chignons. There she is, on the second floor of a nondescript building, a small silhouette stepping into history, accidentally caught by the camera as it pans up.

She is full of life. We see her hopping up and down, although we have only previously seen her frozen in place, in black and white photographs.

She is twelve years old. She has four years left.

These are the only moving pictures of Anne Frank. Silent images, taken from an amateur film made in 1941, doubtless by someone close to the bride or groom. Seven seconds of life—barely a glimpse.

How loved she is, this young Jewish girl who is no longer. The only young Jewish girl who is loved so madly. Anne Frank, imaginary sister to millions of children, who, if she had survived, would be their grandmothers' age. Anne Frank, the eternal adolescent, who today could be my daughter, if people always stayed how old they were when they died.

Anne Frank, whom the world knows so well while knowing very little about her. An image: that of a pale young girl, hair sensibly fastened with a barrette, sitting at her desk, a pen in her hand. A symbol, but of what? Adolescence? The Holocaust? Writing?

What term can we use to refer to her famous diary, which every schoolchild has read and which no adult truly remembers? Is it testimony, evidence, literature? Perhaps it's a deposition from a young girl imprisoned to keep her alive, whose words will eventually break free.

A young girl who, for seven hundred and sixty days, could only travel up and down a staircase, whose entire world was less than forty square meters.

Songs have been dedicated to her, and poems, novels, requiems, and symphonies. Her face has appeared on stamps, mugs, and posters; it has been graffitied on walls and engraved on medallions. Her name can be found on the front of hundreds of schools and libraries and was bestowed on an asteroid in 1995. Her writings have been added to UNESCO's Memory of the World register, alongside the Magna Carta.

In 2021, she made front-page news in the Netherlands: in Amsterdam, opponents of the Covid-19 vaccination passport brandished her portrait, chanting "Freedom, freedom."

Anne Frank: venerated and exploited.

On August 18, 2021, I spent the night at the Anne Frank House, in the museum's Annex.

I went in order to perceive space, since we cannot perceive time. We cannot explain to ourselves the weight of an hour, the density of a week. How to imagine what twenty-five months of life felt like for eight people hidden in this cramped place?

So, all night long, I will pace from one room to another, from her parents' bedroom to the bathroom, from the attic to the small common area, and I will count the steps Anne Frank had available to her. So few steps.

What should we call her? I say *Anne,* but this false intimacy makes me uncomfortable. I can't say *Anne,* something blocks me, a thing that will materialize and make it impossible for me to enter her bedroom. So I say *Anne Frank,* as if taking attendance, as if to call on the once-brilliant student of a phantom junior high. Two syllables.

I thought of the night I would spend there as a kind of meditation, a silence. I imagined the night as a suitable time to acknowledge Anne Frank's absence. I prepared myself to be attuned to the void, to receive it.

I was mistaken. The night was inhabited, lit by reflections; some urgency still dwelled at the heart of the Annex, crouched there, ready to be discovered.

May 2021. Like Paris, Amsterdam is still partly under lockdown. My interview with the director of the museum, Ronald Leopold, takes place on screen. The conversation is crucial: he alone can authorize me to spend the night in the Annex. We talk about this and that, as a way of getting to know each other. Although he is glad Anne Frank and her story still mean something to people, he is sorry that all this adoration overshadows her writing.

Some people come every year, and have done for decades, to commune with her in her room. They leave letters, stuffed animals, rosaries, candles. It is not uncommon for a visitor to refuse to leave the Annex, convinced she is Anne Frank reincarnate.

This degree of identification perplexes the director. Calling her by her first name, as some of his colleagues do, troubles him as well.

Of course, working at the museum every day creates a kind of proximity to her, but Anne Frank is neither a family member nor a friend.

While we're on the subject, he is by no means interested in making me fill out a questionnaire, but he would like to know: what does she represent for me?

I act as if my project were the fruit of a rational decision. I speak in a detached tone about my work, the young girls at the center of my novels: they all challenge the spaces they are allowed to occupy. All of them have seen their stories misinterpreted and rewritten by adults.

I'm improvising.

I don't dare admit the truth, out of fear that Ronald Leopold will take me for a fanatic, obsessed with Anne Frank. I can't explain to him that I don't quite understand the desire for this writing project myself, which has been following me around ever since it showed up a few weeks earlier.

One night in April, two syllables—maybe I even said them in my sleep—slipped out of my childhood.

Anne. Frank.

I hadn't been thinking of her the previous days or been reading anything about her. I barely remember the *Diary.* But during the night, her name emerges. Anne Frank keeps me awake. Nothing can dissipate the subject of Anne Frank during the days that follow. She is the echo of something I'm not quite aware of, yet.

I can't admit to the director that I don't know what exactly she means to me. Still: I have to write this essay.

Even through a screen, my unease must be palpable. Ronald Leopold reassures me there's no need to answer him right away. That very night I write him an email. There are certainly "objective" reasons behind my desire to work on this project: like many children, I was given the *Diary* by my parents, and I began writing to be like her. My mother was hidden as a child during the war. I am Jewish. But I believe that all of that is unimportant, or at least it doesn't quite explain my need to write this text. I finish my letter with a flourish, citing Marguerite Duras: "If we knew anything about what we would write before we did it, before we wrote, we would never write. It wouldn't be worth the trouble." It doesn't take long for him to reply: Ronald Leopold suggests a virtual meeting with a retired academic.

Laureen Nussbaum is one of the last people alive to have known the Franks well, and she is also a pioneer in the field: she's been studying the *Diary* as a work of literature since the 1990s.

On the screen, a lively, elegant woman smiles at me. Laureen knows the question I'm burning to ask. For over sixty years, she's been asked the same one: what was she like as a child, the girl whom Laureen still calls her "little neighbor"?

"Anne was . . . chatty. So chatty! She hated being wrong. The adults found her annoying and adorable at the same time. I was fourteen, Anne was eleven. For me, she was a little kid, my friend Margot's sister. Both of them were very spoiled by their father. He was a modern man, for his time, and he was determined to educate his daughters, for them to form an opinion of the world. They didn't get to see much of it . . ."

Like the Franks, Laureen's parents had to flee Germany in 1933, after the National Socialists' rise to power. They emigrated to the Netherlands, which had remained neutral during the First World War. In Amsterdam, the two families met in Merwedeplein, a neighborhood that was home to many refugees from central Europe.

"After several months, Margot, Anne, and I all spoke fluent Dutch. We played equally with Protestant and Catholic children. We felt as if we had found a haven."

On May 14, 1940, the Dutch surrendered.

The Franks tried to get to the United States, but the Americans demanded so many documents that it was impossible to gather them in time. The borders closed.

* * *

"Little by little, the anti-Jewish measures were put into place. We refused to be cowed by them; we had to keep our heads high. We were no longer allowed to take public transportation or to own a bicycle? We would go on foot. We no longer had the right to go to the cinema or to concerts? Too bad, we'd play music at home. In the summer of 1941, the headteachers at the high schools drew up lists of students 'of Jewish blood.' In class, we were required to sit apart. A short while later, we were forbidden even to attend. Margot was devastated. She would go to wait for her former classmates at the end of the day, she missed them so much.

"Jewish children were no longer permitted to go to school? Never mind, there were very good Jewish teachers; we would make our own schools.

"We held on to whatever joy came our way. Otto rented films that he would project for his daughters; Anne would make tickets, addressing them to her friends. They were perfect reproductions, down to every last detail: the hour of the screening, the seat reservation."

Laureen brings her chair closer to her desk and flips through a book. I recognize Anne Frank's profile on the cover. She adjusts her glasses and clears her voice:

Saturday 20 June 1942

Jews were required to wear a yellow star; Jews were required to turn in their bicycles; Jews were forbidden to use trams; Jews were forbidden to ride in cars, even their own; Jews were required to do their shopping between 3.00 and 5.00 p.m.; Jews were required to frequent only Jewish-owned barbershops and beauty salons; Jews were forbidden to be out on the streets between 8.00 p.m. and 6.00

> a.m.; Jews were forbidden to go to theatres, cinemas or any other forms of entertainment; Jews were forbidden to use swimming pools, tennis courts, hockey fields or any other athletic fields; Jews were forbidden to go rowing; Jews were forbidden to take part in any athletic activity in public; Jews were forbidden to sit in their gardens or those of their friends after 8.00 p.m.; Jews were forbidden to visit Christians in their homes; Jews were required to attend Jewish schools, etc. You couldn't do this and you couldn't do that, but life went on. Jacque always said to me, "I don't dare do anything any more, 'cause I'm afraid it's not allowed."

"This page of the *Diary* is the first to acknowledge something other than her daily life at school. . . . I remember another thing Jews were forbidden to do. Jews were no longer allowed to keep pigeons. The Nazis really thought of everything. . . . The yellow star became obligatory in January 1942. It was so humiliating to be singled out like that, as if we had the plague. I no longer dared leave my home. There were round-ups, the Nazis arrested Jews by the hundreds in the middle of Amsterdam, they forced them to kneel, to . . . do things . . . things that were vile. We knew they were being deported to Mauthausen. Every family was scared of receiving what was being called a 'summons.' The Gestapo sent them to young Jews between the ages of sixteen and forty. They had nine days to declare themselves to the police. Margot and I had just turned sixteen."

On July 6, 1942, Margot didn't go to class. Worried, Laureen went to check on her friend. The door to the apartment was half open. The rooms were empty, the beds unmade.

The night before, a Gestapo agent had rung their doorbell, carrying the much-feared summons: Margot had to take a few of her things and present herself to the convoy that would bring her to a "work camp."

Although Laureen remembers being shaken, she wasn't surprised.

"Mr. Frank had started talking about how he wasn't going to wait around for the Gestapo to arrest them. Everyone thought they'd fled to Switzerland. We could never have imagined that Margot and Anne were so close by, in the same city . . ."

Even today, Laureen calls him Mr. Frank: an elegant man, the director of a small pectin company whose erudition and calm impressed her as a child.

A liberal Jew, with modern ideas about education: as soon as they arrived in the Netherlands, he registered his youngest daughter at the Montessori nursery in Merwedeplein.

A German Jew, an officer in the army during the First World War, who was decorated for acts of bravery. Perhaps, very likely, he thought that would protect him. But for the Nazis, Mr. Frank was a Jew before he was a German.

Laureen wouldn't see him again until 1945, when he returned unrecognizable, skeletal and exhausted, a survivor of Auschwitz-Birkenau and a widower: Edith died at Auschwitz on January 6, 1945.

I'm not recording Laureen Nussbaum; I prefer to take notes. In my notebook, Otto Frank's terrible odyssey is a series of numbers. Five months spent trying to return to Amsterdam.

On January 27, 1945, the Red army entered the death camp. Otto was so weak he couldn't leave until he'd regained some of his strength. In February, the fighting went on in most of Europe; it would have been too dangerous to travel. When Otto Frank finally received the document authorizing him to leave, he had to wait longer still, as the Polish roads had been destroyed.

On March 5th, Otto Frank arrived in Katowice. He stayed for three weeks. On April 1st, he took the train to Odesa, a trip that took four weeks. From there, he managed to get on board a boat bound for Marseille, with some other refugees. In France, he found a train going to Roermond, in the Netherlands. On June 2nd, a car took him from Roermond to Amsterdam.

When he rang at her parents' door one Sunday, Mr. Frank had nowhere to stay, no family, nor the tranquil confidence Laureen had known in him. He was a man lost among the living.

He had to find his daughters; he spoke only of them. He knew they had been deported to Bergen-Belsen. He fixated on their youth: surely they would have survived.

He published an ad in the Dutch newspapers: "Information sought concerning Margot Frank, 19, and Anne Frank, 16, in the January transport to Bergen-Belsen. Tel: 37059."

Every morning, he went to the Red Cross headquarters as soon as it opened. He took a photograph from his pocket: have you perhaps had any news of Margot, or of Anne?

He paced the hospitals: have you seen Anne and Margot? He ran to every train station when the rare survivors from Bergen-Belsen began to arrive. He flagged them down, showed each of them the photograph of his daughters.

Mr. Frank, when he came to lunch at Laureen's parents' house on Sundays, spoke in the future tense, never in the conditional. He said "when I find them."

On July 18, 1945, Otto Frank stopped looking. The letter he'd just received was short, five lines written in the hand of a young nurse at Bergen-Belsen called Janny Brilleslijper.

Janny was deported with her sister Lientje. Both had been in the Resistance and then detained in the camps of Westerbork, Auschwitz, and Bergen-Belsen. Like the Frank sisters.

Janny's letter confirmed the deaths of Otto's two daughters.

* * *

Laureen excuses herself, gets up, and disappears from the screen. I hear a tap running, then the frail silhouette reappears with a glass of water.

I am worried that our conversation is too difficult for her and we agree to speak again another night.

As I am about to sign off, Laureen motions for me to wait: she would like to speak to me a bit about the *Diary*. Some encounters really begin the moment you make to leave, when you are in a hurry to go. That's it, then. It is words that beat at the heart of the essential.

I jot down a few phrases, and then they get lost in the rest of our conversation. Doubtless it is too soon for me to heed Laureen's warning.

This particular evening, she advises that I have a look at the covers of the different editions of the *Diary*. They are extremely revealing, in terms of what the editors have chosen to highlight and, also, the words they avoid using.

In the 1960s, for instance, Laureen tells me, you could find these words: "Reading the *Diary* is like watching a teenager flourish in the face of *adversity*."

When it was published in the United States, Eleanor Roosevelt was asked to write an introduction. She praises the "shining nobility of [the human] spirit" and is moved by its message of hope. The *Diary* is a "monument" erected to all those who "have worked and are working still for peace."

No mention of the Nazi regime, or of the Holocaust. Not a word about the conditions under which Anne Frank wrote.

"Anne wasn't working for peace. She was forestalling death by writing her life. Don't forget that," Laureen Nussbaum counters. "Anne Frank wanted to be read, not deified. Hannah Arendt described the adoration that made her its object as 'cheap sentiment at the expense of a great catastrophe.' She wasn't a saint or a symbol. Her *Diary* is the work of a young girl who was the victim of genocide perpetrated in the face of absolute indifference on the part of all those who knew about it. Please don't use the word *hope*."

Our exchange is a first step in the night. A step into the void, as well, which shows me the extent of my ignorance. The *Diary,* which has sold over thirty million copies worldwide, is not just a journal or an eyewitness account. To reduce it to testimony is to deny Anne Frank her craft, Laureen tells me. Anne wanted to become a writer or a journalist: she *wrote* it.

In my notebook, a series of question marks float around an underlined date: March 29, 1944.

That day, although she had been hiding in the Annex since the summer of 1942, Anne heard an announcement on Radio Oranje made by the Dutch minister of education, from his exile in London. He asked the Dutch to keep their letters and their diaries: after the war, these writings would be precious testimony. This declaration galvanized her, she was excited, she told her father about it: her diary could be published, one day.

Immediately she set to work revising it. She abandoned the spontaneous tone of the early pages and polished the style. She drafted a prologue, cutting some passages that struck her as too personal and expanding others. She decided to use pseudonyms, turning the occupants of the Annex, whom she often sketched crudely, into characters. She chose a particular narrative form, addressing an imaginary friend called Kitty, the heroine of the young adult novels she devoured. She described the Annex with great detail, room by room, and gave precise historical context.

She scrutinized sentences, questioned the relevance of her chapters, listened to the rhythm of a paragraph, moved from an introspective tone to more political observations. From now on, Anne was not only a young girl keeping a diary but an author thinking of her future readers. When she started the diary on June 12, 1942, she had no particular idea of its being read, but, beginning in March 1944, although she wrote *I,* she began to think of *us.* She was persuaded her writing would have a future, that it would seek us out; today, it sought *me* out.

What can we call her book, which I elected not to reread before my night in the Annex? It is a stocktaking, which we are invited to witness. We approach its conclusion apprehensively, knowing that after the Franks were arrested on August 4th, there will be no more words. We know how it ends.

Its author did not.

In early June, I receive an email with the subject line "Security/ Anne Frank House" informing me that I have been given permission to spend the night of August 18th in the Annex. I will not be permitted to eat or drink, or to take any photographs.

Some of the security requirements are typical for a museum; others, however, are more surprising: "The Annex is part of the museum display. It is not permitted to suspend bags or clothing from the doorknobs, or to use the outlets to charge a telephone. The stairway is steep and its steps are unequal: sturdy, comfortable shoes are advised, preferably without leather soles."

I will be alone in the Annex. The night guard will be in the contemporary museum. I will have to leave at seven in the morning.

I know, I have read, that the place where I will spend ten hours is an empty apartment. Visitors process past this absence. It is this void that transforms this apartment into a museum. The void is addressed to us, a plea from a man who is no longer here: Otto Frank, who, when he returned from Auschwitz in 1945, found their hiding place pillaged by the Nazis. They ransacked every inch of it, even the most insignificant cupboards or drawers or shelves.

Otto Frank, who, when the idea of turning the Annex into a museum was put to him in 1960, required that the apartment be left in exactly the state in which he had found it. For us to witness the void, without being able to turn away from it. For us to be confronted by it.

To see an emptiness that can never be filled.

That way, on our way out, we wouldn't be able to say: I saw nothing in the Annex. We will say: in the Annex, there is *nothing,* and what I saw there is *nothing.*

I will spend the night in this place where for twenty-five months, eight people submitted themselves to silence, learning all the forms it could take, from whispers to muffled steps to total immobility.

Anne Frank's everyday life was that of a prisoner with a life sentence. Life in the Annex was one of permanent constraint.

At eight o'clock, the employees arrived at their office, located just beneath the hideout. Five of them were aware of the Franks' presence—they gave them food and books and encouragement—but the storekeepers were not. And so, until 12:30 p.m., "No running water, no flushing toilet, no walking around, no noise whatsoever," wrote Anne Frank. They then had an hour to eat lunch, go to the toilet, listen to the news on Radio Oranje, chat among themselves. At 1:30, they resumed their immobility. They would read, write, anything that could help them forget the back cramps, the obsessive heaviness of a full bladder.

In the Annex, the body is deprived of light, of air, of movement. Worn out, hunched over, numb. Starving and queasy, sickened by too much starchy food and rotten potatoes. A body subject to every kind of fear and worry, for danger is everywhere: people live in the building on the right, and the one on the left is a carpentry workshop.

Can you get used to living with danger?

Does fear suddenly take hold of you, like a riptide—a force that drags you out to sea, no use struggling against it? Or is it a slow drip, day after day? In the end, do you get used to being afraid?

Their worries accumulate, and haunt them. They are afraid of being exposed. Of accidentally ruffling the opaque fabric Anne Frank and her father nailed to the windows the day they arrived. Afraid of getting sick, of not managing to stifle a sneeze or a coughing fit. Of not being able to see a doctor.

Their hearts pound at the slightest unusual noise, like the day they heard burglars breaking into the office downstairs.

They are afraid of being burned alive, on the nights when the bombs fall too close to the Annex. Afraid of dying crushed beneath the rubble—they can't escape to a bomb shelter. Afraid that they won't be able to stand it, shut up like this with seven other people, with no privacy at all. Afraid they'll lose their minds, and lose all hope—but what hope is there. Afraid, as well, of being betrayed by one of their employees or protectors. The fear, the terror, the anguish of knowing what would befall them if they were to be discovered. What will befall them, when they are discovered.

"Not being able to go outside," writes Anne Frank on September 28, 1942, "upsets me more than I can say, and I'm terrified our hiding place will be discovered and that we'll be shot. That, of course, is a fairly dismal prospect."

Fear, she writes on November 8, 1943, is "a dark mass of clouds, so that we can go neither up nor down. It looms before us like an impenetrable wall, trying to crush us, but not yet able to."

A few weeks before leaving for Amsterdam, I read a bit, as I always do before embarking on a new project. Accruing bits of information—a timid approach to my "subject"—is how I warm up. It's also a means of putting off writing, waiting until it becomes urgent.

I read as if I'm tracing a circle around a central point, without getting too close to it; as if I'm getting ready to enter a labyrinth. I read scholarly articles that reflect on the difference between an imprint and a trace, I reread Patrick Modiano's *Dora Bruder,* I read a biography of Audrey Hepburn, whose mother worshipped Hitler; the actress turned down the chance to play Anne Frank in the film, concerned that she didn't have the "legitimacy" to do it.

I read a book about the way trauma of the Holocaust is passed down over several generations; I read a biography of Miep Gies, Otto Frank's secretary, one of the five employees who helped hide the Franks. I read feminist analyses of the *Diary,* including one by Laureen Nussbaum. I read one of Philip Roth's early novels, *The Ghost Writer,* in which he imagines Anne Frank as an adult, an Anne Frank who survived, hiding behind a pseudonym in the United States. On YouTube, there are hundreds of videos paying tribute to her, many of which use the theme song of the movie *Titanic* as a soundtrack. Some comments have been removed for hate speech.

At night I'm like an imposter who is about to be unmasked. I dream that I have to sit an exam, which I fail; I dream I'm refused entry to the museum.

As the date of my departure nears, my anxiety turns to doubt, and then to certainty: I am not the right person to write this book. How can I write about something I have so assiduously avoided?

Ever since my teenage years, I have looked away, declining to watch documentaries about the Holocaust or read books about it. I walked out of the cinema during *Schindler's List;* I was nauseated by Benigni's *Life Is Beautiful.* I couldn't stand to see the Holocaust romanticized.

My brain gets muddled anytime anyone even raises the subject of the Holocaust. In high school, I avoided courses on the Second World War. I don't need to read or watch films about it: I *know* how this story goes. I *know* what happened to the people who somewhere around 1920 had to flee certain death in the pogroms, the ghettos, in Russia, in Poland. People who embraced their mothers, fathers, brothers, and sisters, without knowing if they would ever see each other again, who left everything behind. They gave up their names, their hopes and dreams, and their mother tongues, and not by choice. Citizenship would never be an uncomplicated affair.

I *know* these families' stories, brought up to love a fictional country, the France of Victor Hugo, Jean Jaurès, and the Declaration of the Rights of Man. I know that instead of finding safe haven, they were humiliated, hounded, deported.

Maybe it would be better to say I *understand* this story, which is also my family's story. To *know* implies that I have been told it, that it has been transmitted to me. But a story that is missing entire paragraphs can't be told. And the story that I *understand* is a narrative ridden with silences, which the third generation after the Shoah, that is to say my own, has inherited.

Our family trees have been torn up, burned, carbonized. The story breaks off.

Words have proved impotent, have slipped away from these families, from my family. The untellable story goes in circles, never punctuated, never finished.

These lines are frayed, haunted by so many dead we don't even know how they died. Gassed, burned, or thrown, naked, into a mass grave, forever denied a gravestone. We can't pay homage to them. We can't close the chapter.

In these families, everything is conjugated in terms of *never again.* There are countries we'll never return to—Poland, Russia—lands of persecution. There are languages we'll never speak again.

These families have only known extremes. Exile or death. Heroism or death. To be born *after* is to live perpetually in debt. Every child will be seen as a miracle. They will bear the duty of surviving.

It is impossible to grasp my great-uncle's bravery; it leaves you speechless. A Polish Jew, a member of the Resistance and the FTP-MOI, these young people—stateless, or Ashkenazi immigrants—these underground soldiers carried out guerrilla warfare against the Nazis, a near-daily fight.

It is impossible to grasp, it leaves you speechless, what another great-uncle endured, the one with the purple numbers tattooed on his wrist, his ID number at Auschwitz-Birkenau.

It leaves you speechless, my mother's childhood; there is no way to cure her of it. A little girl who was hidden to save her life, a child who knew, at four years old, that being Jewish was a death sentence. A child who, on her way home from school one day, rounded a corner and came upon the mutilated bodies and bashed-in skulls of murdered teenage Jews.

It leaves you speechless, the desperate rage of those who came *after.*

That of a cousin, born too late to fight, in 1944; from the barricades of 1968 to the guerrillas of South America, he never stopped looking for a war. He wrote in his autobiography that to be born Jewish is to come "from death," and, no sooner born, one must prepare oneself "to return" to it. He wrote that "it made no sense to be young if you weren't risking violent death," and his wish would be brutally granted. He would get several bullets in the back, courtesy of a gang of fascist police officers, shot down in the middle of Paris in 1979.

Other members of the family, closer to my age, fell into a permanent stupor, turning their daily lives into a chemical cocoon of antidepressants and tranquilizers. In my family, devastation is as hereditary as eye color.

During my adolescence, I avoided the history of the Jews of central Europe. I turned my back on the void. I didn't want to hear about it, didn't want to know about it. Their nightmares would not be my own. All I wanted was to be part of a *normal* family, who didn't have history books written about them, who inspired neither pity nor hatred.

In middle school, I was infatuated with the girls who wore little gold crosses around their necks. They were so marvelously *normal.* They were so carefree, so nonchalant when they talked about Sunday school, their upcoming first communions. In high school, I envied the ones who had robust family trees, in which people died for banal reasons, like illness or old age. I fell in love with men who had known their great-grandfathers. I fell in love with women who came from families so big they had to rent a house big enough to fit them all at Christmas gatherings.

I was fascinated by their sideboards, decorated with old family photos, by any trace of the past, really—tablecloths, recipes inherited from a great-grandmother. The conventional after-dinner conversations, which centered around who looked like who in the family, made me uncomfortable. I didn't know who I looked like. My grandparents didn't have any pictures of their brothers and sisters, those Russian and Polish teenagers who died of hunger, of exposure, of exhaustion, in the convoys that led them to the concentration camp at Auschwitz-Birkenau and in the camp itself.

* * *

Even my literary preferences betrayed my refusal to belong to this history: I was devoted to whichever authors resembled me the least, with whom I had absolutely nothing in common. They brandished their magnificent superficiality, their elegant torments, their pop decadence—the subtleties of Françoise Sagan's sadness delighted me, as did the glittering conjugal drama of F. Scott Fitzgerald, and I was captivated by a film called "Christiane F., 13 ans, droguée, prostituée," who wandered the streets to a soundtrack of David Bowie.

I loathed the kinds of movies where you left the theatre with your eyes all red; I made fun of my friends for crying at *Sophie's Choice.*

Only the deaths of animals moved me; I cried my eyes out if I heard about a dog who'd been run over or a wounded horse who'd had to be shot after a race. Human suffering left me indifferent; violent death was perhaps too familiar. I use the word in its most immediate sense: being put to death ran in the family.

I'd rather be dancing, announced the poster pinned on my bedroom wall.

I'd rather dance than hear the echo of death. I wanted to be made new, reborn from my own choices: no one, in the family, had ever studied ballet.

Maurice Béjart said that a dancer had to be part nun and part boxer.

Ballet was my religion, it smelled like rosin and sweat. I had found my world: there we suffered in silence.

I devoted myself to perpetuating the illusion of lightness. I recopied bits of Théophile Gautier in a notebook—*sculpt, smooth, chisel*; he had co-written the libretto of my favorite ballet, *Giselle.* I cherished my teachers' humiliating sternness, their orders—"again!"—gave a shape and rhythm to my days.

I looked down on other people my age, who hung out in the cafés after school. They had nothing to fight against; such an easy life was meaningless. Whereas dancers had to contend daily with gravity, fatigue, pain.

Ballet was a place of cruelty and competition but it was cordoned off from politics, a museum made of tulle. A world in which men were princes and women ghosts, *wilis,* spirits of young dead women who, the legend went, haunted those who betrayed their promises. I was betraying my family's past, but I had made no promises.

When asked where I was from, I sifted through different answers to find the one that seemed most acceptable.

I made vague mention of my Russian and Polish origins; my blond hair meant people didn't ask any further questions. I omitted one word from the accounts I gave of myself, but what did it matter, it was such a small word, and it was way too loaded: *Jew.* I refrained from uttering it.

I said that I was "from everywhere" and it was partly true: I grew up in Bulgaria and Romania, where I had so loved celebrating Orthodox Easter. My grandparents were Polish and Russian, but also French, from the Southwest, on my father's side; I spent my holidays in the Landes. Another part of my family was from North America; I was trilingual.

When I spoke English, people thought I was American. When I spoke Romanian, they thought I was Romanian. It was a game I liked to play on Saturday afternoons: roam around Paris like a tourist, asking for directions in English, as if I were someone else. I had no accent, nowhere I belonged.

I am undoubtedly a child of the 1980s, the heyday of "self-reinvention," a dream made possible through your VCR. Aerobics promised you a new body, and self-help books a new personality. To become the person you'd always dreamed of, you just had to want it. *Just do it.*

Identity was a costume, a disguise.

Madonna was Everywoman, a Marilyn, a Virgin, a feminist, a businesswoman, a sex symbol, a fashion goddess, a dancer, a mother, Eva Perón, an unnatural blond, proud of having created and then re-created herself.

Music sold optimism on a global level: "We Are the World," a new world in which no one had to go hungry or cold; you just had to believe in it. Racism was on the wane, thanks to a little yellow hand grabbing the lapel of your jacket. Hands off my friend, indeed.*

And I believed it wholeheartedly, hoping to distance myself from a devastated landscape, from *all those dead people.*

I joined all the groups, fought for all the causes, especially the ones that didn't directly concern me: the Zapatistas in Chiapas, Basque prisoners, or the unhoused. All the injustices, all the tragedies, except *one.*

* The slogan of the group SOS Racisme, launched in 1985, is Touche pas à mon pote—hands off my friend, or hands off my pal/buddy. The logo was printed on a yellow hand held up as if to say *Stop,* and people wore them as lapel pins.—Trans.

Memory is a series of doorways, which we can open or ignore; memory, wrote Louise Bourgeois, "is meaningless if you seek it out; you have to wait till it attacks you."

Before entering the night that August of 2021, I don't *know* much, except for this: ghosts, who have a reputation for pitiless haunting, know how to behave. They wait for us; they have all the time that we lack.

They are waiting for us to be ready for their disruption. For our eyes to open, for us to learn, over time, to perceive their patient shadows, so we can make room for those we are accustomed to calling *lost.* That is when we will be reunited with them.

On August 16, 2021, I am struck with a brutal fever, a childhood fever.

Laid up in bed, I send an email to Alina Gurdiel, my editor: I'm so sorry but I'm not going to be able to go to Amsterdam. I feel a twinge of relief; my friends were right—it's not exactly the most lighthearted of projects.

The morning I'm supposed to leave, the fever is gone. I will go to Amsterdam.

In the train, a woman sitting behind me is becoming agitated during a telephone call. It's too vague, you are too vague, she tells her correspondent. I imagine them, on the other side of the line, trying desperately to use more specific language, to refine their point.

I would like to grab the phone from her and comfort this vague person. They are an endangered species in a world that demands transparency. We value clarity, the clarity of a media campaign. Being able to summarize your thoughts in a few words is a contemporary skill, the real estate agent's dream.

Clarity is the domain of the public speaker, the politician or the public relations manager. We can see through them: they're trying to sell us something. Vagueness provokes our curiosity: we have to take a closer look. It's the sea mist that conceals the profile of a cliff. It's the infatuation we feel at the beginning of a love affair, before it has crystallized into a *relationship.* It's a sadness with no cause, which rises up when we least expect it, at the edge of happiness. Vague creatures belong to the realm of fiction, which thrives on beings who always remain somewhat knowable. A novel can't be transparent; it is a weave of doubts and solitude, that of the writer who devoted all her time to it. A novel doesn't sell us something; it *suggests.*

The writers we love are all so vague. Georges Perec isn't pretending otherwise, when he tries to define Judaism:

> it isn't a sign of belonging,
> it doesn't have to do with belief, or religion, or a code
> of behavior, a way of life, or a language;
> it seems more like a silence, a deficiency, a question,
> a questioning, a dubiousness, an uneasiness:
>
> an uneasy certainty, and looming behind that, another certainty,
> abstract, oppressive, and intolerable:
> that of having been labeled a Jew,
> Jew therefore victim,
> and so beholden for being alive to exile and luck

Behind me, the woman ends the conversation with a question that cannot be answered. She sighs: can't you be a bit more clear?

Amsterdam is turning its back on summer and submitting to different forms of autumnal rain.

At the hotel, the desk manager is most accommodating, providing me with a list of the best coffee shops and clubs with ladies-only lap dances, as well as a discount for a guided tour of the city. There are choices: the art museums take half a day; the Anne Frank option is much shorter, only a two-hour walk. You can retrace her steps through the city: see her favorite park, her primary school, and, of course, the museum, in which can be found her "little hiding place." The young man pronounces these last few words with a childish pleasure.

What time would you like to have breakfast?

I'm sure I'll be sleeping in tomorrow morning, I tell him. Because tonight, I am going to see Anne Frank, that is, the museum. He nods his head impassively, very good, Madame.

The room in which I will not spend the night is spacious and calm. Someone has left a welcome note on the bed, in English: "You'll be surprised!"

Turn it over and the note promises: "Here, you'll forget everything!"

Can I complain to reception if the promise turns out to be a lie, if, in the morning, I haven't forgotten everything? Does the hotel keep a register of everything we don't manage to leave behind, of all the intractable, nagging memories?

* * *

I have a meeting at three o'clock with one of the curators, Teresien da Silva, in the neighborhood of Merwedeplein. She will show me the apartment where the Franks lived from 1933 to 1942.

The red brick building with white shutters is much like all the others, except for a discreet tribute on the sidewalk: brass plaques informing us that here once lived Otto, Edith, Margot, and Anne Frank.

Teresien expresses herself with a researcher's precision, in facts and figures. She has spoken with over ninety witnesses, friends, or relatives of the Franks; she has worked at the museum for thirty-seven years. She knows Laureen Nussbaum, and she had the honor of knowing Miep Gies very well.

Once inside, the apartment echoes with our presence; our voices seem too loud, almost intrusive. Teresien busies herself in the kitchen, making us some tea. I don't dare sit on the old-fashioned armchair in the sitting room, or anywhere else. I am visiting the *Franks.*

Seeing my unease, Teresien reassures me that I can sit wherever I like. This is not the original furniture, only copies. The apartment isn't a museum but a residency for writers fleeing persecution in their home countries. Here, they can write, they can live.

We walk from room to room, as if we were contemplating buying the place, or as if we were deep in the folds of History, visiting a museum after all.

The apartment was pillaged in August 1944, a few days after the family was deported. Nothing remained.

Restoring it required meticulous research, Teresien explains; they had to scrutinize the Franks' family photographs and speak to their neighbors and friends, who might remember a table or a rug.

Teresien praises her team's tenacity. Take the lamp, for instance, in Anne Frank's bedroom. In this photograph of the young girl sitting at her desk, you can see it reflected in the mirror. We looked at it through a loupe, we blew up the picture, and we showed it to dealers in antiques and secondhand furniture.

The wallpaper was easier: at the time, renters changed it when they moved. Several families had followed the Franks. Their wallpaper was peeled back, and, strip by strip, they uncovered the right pattern, which they were able to scan and print.

We are looking at what *she* looked at, when she was writing, Teresien proudly tells me.

This attentive process of reconstruction puts me ill at ease. Everything here wants to be as authentic as possible, and yet none of it is, except for this oppressive feeling of absence. It is a constant hum, strident, obsessive.

The Franks' apartment is the set for a play without actors, a museum without visitors. As the philosopher Sybille Krämer writes, "In the mark left behind by an imprint . . . we can see that someone or something has passed through. The presence of the trace attests to the absence that formed it. Traces do not allow us to see what is absent, but absence itself."*

Everything in Anne's bedroom appears frozen in time, interrupted; the smallest of objects seems to await her return. The narrow bed carefully made up, sheets pulled tight. The half-open drawers of the dresser. The dark wood of the desk on which have

* S. Krämer, "Was also ist eine Spur? Und worin besteht ihre epistemologische Rolle? Eine Bestandsaufnahme" [What Is a Trace? And What Is Its Epistemological Role? A Stocktaking], in *Spur. Spurenlesen als Orientierungstechnik und Wissenskunst* [The Trace: Reading Traces as Navigation Technique and Knowledge Art], ed. S. Krämer, W. Kogge, and G. Grube (Frankfurt am Main: Suhrkamp, 2007), pp. 11–33.—Trans.

been placed blank sheets of paper on which no one will ever write. Anne Frank is painfully missing from her childhood bedroom.

Teresien invites me to follow her upstairs. We take a staircase so steep it is practically a ladder. The writer-in-residence lives here.

In 1933, it was sublet, and its resident shared the Franks' kitchen and bathroom; that was the custom.

Was it their father who took their pictures? Sweet Margot is fourteen; she is squinting in the bright sun, in a two-piece bathing suit with red polka dots, her longish brown hair pulled back with a barrette. Standing slightly knock-kneed, she seems in a hurry to get the picture over with.

Anne, however, poses eagerly. Stretched out on a lounge chair, wearing a short-sleeved blouse and checkered shorts, she smiles. Between her hands she holds a straw hat that is much too big for her. If a photograph is a permanent image, this one has immortalized the radiance of a joyful summer's day.

How reliably these fleeting joys spill out of us, when we're twelve. If we hear a funny joke on the radio we let out a snort; if the teacher scolds us at school we mock his frown, his knitted brow. We are barely able to restrain our excitement at the idea of meeting up with a friend after school.

How they make our hearts seize up, these everyday joys of a final summer. The summer when Otto Frank was preparing their escape.

When did Otto Frank finally realize that the faith he had placed in their adoptive country was a tragic mistake?

The Dutch are not only willing to carry out the occupying power's orders but are actively participating in putting in place anti-Jewish measures.

As early as September 1940, the Nazis exclude Jews from public office and the liberal professions: the economy must be "de-Jewified."

In 1941, to avoid having his company seized, Otto Frank officially cedes his directorship to his secretary's husband, Jan Gies, and to his friend Johannes Kleiman. In reality, Otto Frank continues to make all key decisions.

Every day, he goes to his office on foot; he is no longer permitted to take public transport. But walking across Amsterdam is dangerous: in February 1941, the German police arrested four hundred Jewish men, brutally rounding them up—including several of Otto Frank's friends.

In January 1942, he is forced to sew a yellow star onto the lapel of his jacket. Four capital letters designate him as a target: JOOD. The star is obligatory and it is not free: it costs one clothing coupon plus four centimes.

Otto Frank knows they'll have to leave, and soon. But where can they go?

The Otto Frank that Teresien evokes for me is a man faced with extraordinary decisions. And yet his life had not prepared him for such radical change; he had grown up solidly middle class and was well over forty when the Nazis took power in Germany.

He will dream up, and implement, a chance at survival: instead of running from the danger, the family will hide in the middle of the city that is hunting them.

This choice has been seen as a controversial one; some historians say that he should have agreed to be separated from his daughters, that if he had sent them somewhere else, they might have survived. That in trying to protect them, he had condemned them to death.

Teresien has no patience for these "should haves" and "shouldn't haves." In the Franks' kitchen where we are drinking our tea, she lets slip the even tone of a researcher and asks: and where would he have sent the girls? Who did he know in the countryside, this German immigrant, this city dweller? Some Dutch families were agreeing to hide people in their chicken coops, exposed to the cold, or in little shacks in the forest, built quickly and on the cheap. They saw it as an opportunity to make a little money.

Anne and Margot would have been completely dependent on strangers, easy prey, preyed on sexually, as well. Otto Frank did what he could, with what he could.

For months, he makes lists. He doesn't want to forget anything, when the family moves into the empty rooms above the Opetka offices. He has to anticipate all their needs: pots, sheets, soap, matches, candles, aspirin, cough medicine. Should he take his daughters' schoolbooks and dictionaries, so they can study? How many months will they spend there? One autumn? Longer? Will they need winter clothes?

Every morning, Otto leaves the apartment in Merwedeplein with a frying pan, or bath towels, hidden in his bag; every morning, he risks being stopped by the Nazis who are spread out all over Amsterdam. The apartment that Otto is slowly emptying is the last bright space they will occupy, before their disappearance into darkness and silence.

Teresien accompanies me to the front steps; the rain has stopped. She smiles, apologizes for not being able to spend more time with me; there is so much to do at the museum. Emboldened, I ask her: after thirty-seven years spent with the Franks, does she feel a particular affinity with any one of them in particular?

Margot is the one she finds most moving. She's there in the background of History, discreet, an extra. She also kept a journal. Who knows, maybe one day we'll find it . . .

We say goodbye, and I look at the building one last time. The windows to the apartment are open.

For the Franks, until July 6, 1942, these are ordinary windows, opened wide every morning to a blend of everyday urban smells: hot asphalt, toast, gasoline. Windows that can be closed to avoid a draft. When you're shut up in a closed space for twenty-five months, do you feel nostalgic for the breeze? Do you even remember it? Was it like a breath, or more like a whisper?

I didn't take any notes during my visit to the Franks' apartment, and now, in the café where I've pitched up, I'm afraid of forgetting something essential. Maybe it's nerves about the evening ahead.

How to judge what is essential? Is it obvious or do we have to flush it out? And what if everything in the Merwedeplein apartment were essential? In the smallest, silent corner; in the middle of every empty room, where they no longer live.

Today, this word belongs to the publicists; it's a women's magazine word: "what's essential for spring."

But for Anne Frank, what did it mean when, on July 5, 1942, her parents let her know that Margot has received her much-feared summons? They are going to have to leave as early as the next morning: she can only take the essentials.

Is it possible for a thirteen-year-old to take stock of her short existence in less than one afternoon and to classify it into two categories, *essential* and *nonessential*? Can a thirteen-year-old see her life through the logic of subtraction—taking away the nonessential, a game, a book, a sweater, a cat, Moortje, to whom Anne Frank was so deeply attached.

In the confusion, she would take "curlers, handkerchiefs, schoolbooks, a comb and some old letters."

Though I can't know what she hesitated over, I know, we know, that she decided to take the notebook with the red and white plaid cover and the little brass lock that her father gave her, in which she would write:

> It was a great shock to me, a call-up; everyone knows what that means, I picture concentration camps and lonely cells.

Sunday, July 6, 1942, at 7:30 a.m., a thirteen-year-old girl crosses the gray rainy city. She has slipped onto the wrong side of the law; she is fleeing, her heart racing beneath her yellow star, her thin body bundled up in layers of clothing, enough to last an autumn, a winter, and however many seasons more to come.

> I had on two vests, three pairs of pants, a dress, on top of that a skirt, jacket, summer coat, two pairs of stockings, lace-up shoes, woolly cap, scarf, and still much more. . . . So we walked through the pouring rain, Daddy, Mummy and I, each with a school satchel and shopping bag filled to the brim with all kinds of things thrown together anyhow.

It is eight o'clock in the evening. The museum is closed. The director meets me in the entryway; he lets me in and I leave the daylight behind.

I expected to walk through an old building but instead we are passing through the immaculate rooms of the contemporary museum, built in the late 1990s. Ronald Leopold describes the historical documents on show there, but I retain nothing of this whirlwind tour. If to read Anne Frank's journal is to enter the Annex *alongside her* on the 6th of July 1942, the museum prefers to slowly travel back in time. It prepares the visitor progressively: the modern lighting of the early rooms softens; the smooth polished paintings give way to cracked wood-paneled walls.

An arrow points to a temporary exhibition dedicated to the photographs pasted up on Anne Frank's bedroom walls. Reflexively I make a note in my phone: go see the exhibition. Ronald Leopold is amused: I will certainly be able to find the time, tonight, to stop by.

A steep staircase leads to the offices of the Opetka employees who *knew*; the director uses the word *benefactors*.

Miep and Jan Gies, Bep Voskuijl, Johannes Kleiman, Victor Kugler. What else can we call them?

Defiant? Helpful? Righteous? Idealistic? Reckless?

Though they looked after the family's physical survival, they were also *essential* for morale. Victor Kugler, Otto's righthand man, brought Anne her favorite cinema magazines. Bep enrolled in a Latin class on Margot's behalf. Bep and Miep gave the Frank sisters secretarial work to keep them busy. Jan and Miep borrowed books for them at the library.

Every morning, Miep went up to the Annex, to ask if there were any errands that needed running. In her autobiography, she describes the way Anne pounced on her the minute she heard the door open: Miep! Any news? What's happening outside?

She wanted to know everything, even what the adults don't want to hear about: the round-ups, the arrests, the disappearances, the deportations.

"We can't say we didn't know": the phrase has become a cliché, rendered meaningless by the deluge of information overwhelming us every day. We know. We've seen pictures of every massacre. We have been in attendance at every conflict, as if at a performance.

We can't say we didn't know; we can say we didn't know what to do with what we knew. We can talk about the crushing impotence that takes hold of us; the more we know, the less we can do. The things we witness are like questions asked of us. We can choose not to answer.

I didn't do anything, children cry when they're unjustly accused. I didn't do anything, grown-ups tell themselves as they go about their days.

Miep, Jan, Bep, and Victor knew about the anti-Jewish measures they saw, daily, in the streets of Amsterdam, acts of anti-Semitism.

It would have been easy for them to just keep walking; none of them were Jewish. They had every reason in the world to just keep walking; you could be put in prison for helping Jews, at the very least. After the war, when they were asked why they did what they did, they could only answer in the negative: they couldn't not do what they did.

Miep Gies hated to be talked about as if she were a heroine. She was nothing special, she would say. Otto Frank had hired her as a secretary. He was very respectful of her work. She was always welcome at the Franks' house; they regularly invited her to dinner in the apartment in Merwedeplein; she was very affectionate toward Anne and Margot.

When the first anti-Jewish measures were announced, she had hoped the Franks would be able to flee.

The first morning she saw the yellow star stitched to Otto Frank's overcoat, she was stunned that he greeted her and went to his office as if nothing were awry.

A few weeks later, he told her about his secret plan. She was also stunned by his confidence.

Those who went into hiding were struck from the civil register; they no longer had access to the coupons obtained by presenting their identity cards. The family needed Miep in order to eat. Otto insisted she take time to think before responding. Miep didn't think for a moment of refusing, and neither did her husband.

Was she afraid? Constantly. Afraid of getting sick and not being able to help the people in hiding, afraid of raising the suspicions of other people who worked in the office but didn't know. Afraid, every day, of not finding enough to eat, and also afraid of being denounced by the shopkeepers who might wonder why she was buying such great quantities of food. Afraid of what would happen to her if she were arrested. And afraid, if the Nazis tortured her, of not being able to withstand the pain, of giving everything away.

* * *

None of the protectors liked to brag about their courage. Maybe they were right: courage is a response to danger at a particular moment. Their courage, then, is plural: these were courages, an array of courages, the daily courages of morning and evening for two years, every time they opened the door to the hiding place.

There is madness in the story of the Annex, the madness of recklessness. The beautiful recklessness of the protectors who risked their lives for the Franks.

But also the mad, beautiful recklessness of Otto Frank, at the moment he decided to trust Miep Gies.

These mad beautiful immense acts of recklessness lead to other, further acts of recklessness. Barely a week after they moved to the Annex, Otto and Edith took in Hermann van Pels, his wife, Augusta, and their fifteen-year-old son, Peter. Hermann had worked for Otto since 1939.

Four months later, the anti-Jewish round-ups intensified; the protectors and their charges together selected an eighth person; "the danger is no less for seven people than for eight," said Otto. Fritz Pfeffer, a German Jewish dentist and friend of the Franks', joined them: he fled Germany after Kristallnacht.

Recklessness is something like a reflection produced by generosity. Perhaps that is the *essential* part of this story.

The night turns back time; it seems to me that I have walked several kilometers behind the director. Flights of stairs empty onto long, narrow corridors, which, in turn, give onto still more flights of stairs.

I am expecting the famous pivoting bookcase that hides the entry to the Annex, having seen it many times in photographs. At the end of the next hallway, there it is: stuffed with files, the imitation of a bookshelf behind which a book, a body of work, was created. Marks have been recently added to the floor to indicate a one-meter distance between each visitor.

A few uneven steps lead to a narrow room, shared by Margot and her parents. The director has chosen to install my camp bed here. He thought that Anne's room, right next door, would be a bit too, well . . . It is very *inhabited,* he adds, before slipping out.

I unpack my things. My laptop, a notebook and my diary, a charger, a thermos, a t-shirt, a toothbrush and toothpaste, earplugs (but who is going to disturb me here?) and some Lexomil my mother gave me. Back in my hotel room, I hesitated over whether to pack some pajamas. They're just a bit of stagecraft: I know I am not going to sleep very much here. If at all.

I plan the night. I sketch large columns in my notebook, I organize the time into hourly increments. I list things to do as if I were a tourist here; I circle, on the map of the museum, the documents I have to be sure not to miss, the rooms to visit. I've thought of everything except the temperature: it's freezing. I curse myself for not having brought a sweater; everyone knows they keep the temperature really low in museums to protect the works held there. But what are they protecting here? The Annex is the emptiest museum in the world: only the framed portraits of Edith, Otto, and Margot look out at me from the wall, and a map of the Normandy coast, stuck with multicolored pins—Otto was listening to radio reports about the Allied advance.

From my place on the camp bed, in the half-dark I can make out a narrow rectangle of wallpaper, protected by a frame. From afar, the frame looks empty.

"Often to understand, we have to look into emptiness." Antonioni's phrase is cited in *La Paix avec les morts* [Peace with the Dead], by Rithy Panh and Christophe Bataille. I copied it into my notebook a few days before entering the night.

I go to have a closer look at the framed wallpaper and in the emptiness I can make out some numbers and some faint lines, very straight. In this emptiness a father inscribed, every month, in pencil, his proof of life. Otto Frank noted here that in two years, Margot grew one centimeter and Anne thirteen.

When he returned, alone, from Auschwitz, Otto Frank spent hours in the Annex. He carefully peeled back this rectangle of wallpaper. He could not lose this, too. The only thing left to him were these light gray pencil lines, proof that in this sunless, springless, windless place, life reclaimed a few centimeters from the dark.

The bells of Westerkerk reverberate in unison with the gentle hum of the air conditioning. It is ten o'clock. A few minutes ago, a security guard knocked at the door. She came to bring me a walkie-talkie, which she shows me how to use.

If I leave the bedroom, I have to take it with me, and my phone as well; the Annex is a maze for someone unfamiliar with it. But not to worry, there are surveillance cameras in all the rooms. Gladys will be able to find me if I get lost.

Writing took place between these walls, behind these closed, opaque windows, as protective as they were suffocating. It's a jail, a trap, but also the place where something was born.

These walls witnessed a "bundle of contradictions," as Anne Frank writes on the last page of her diary: those of a teenager, but also of a writer confronting her work. Doubting, questioning. "I'm my best and harshest critic. I know what's good and what isn't."

She is unsparing with herself: of her short story "Cady's Life," she writes that while some of it is good, "as a whole it's nothing special."

One evening in July, Miep surprises Anne in her bedroom, and finds her hunched over her notebook. "I saw a look on her face at this moment that I'd never seen before. It was a look of dark concentration, as if she had a throbbing headache. This look pierced me, and I was speechless. She was suddenly another person there writing at the table," Miep wrote in her autobiography.

In fencing, *engagement* refers to making contact with the opponent's blade.

Writing is engaging in a sword fight. We write as if engaged in an imaginary army, in which we are at once general and foot soldier.

To reread every morning what we have written the night before is much like a dancer's warm-up at the barre in front of the mirror: an exercise in humility. The text is pitiless; it shows us ourselves, like a reflection; it is clumsy, limping, messy. But getting depressed about it is no proof of rigor; it has merely bruised our ego. We are disappointed; we believed ourselves more brilliant than that. Rereading our work without indulgence requires, perhaps, that we "get free of ourselves," as Foucault put it: the text is more important than its author.

Why do we prefer the solitude of writing? Why do we devote so much of our time to unreal—though nevertheless true—lives, to beings who are neither dead nor alive?

Writing is not exactly a choice; it's an avowal of impotence. We write because we don't know any other way to lay hold of reality. Life without writing doesn't suit me, like some overly loose garment in which I've entangled myself. Sometimes we have to contract space to hear the echo of life.

Why do we write? Maybe it's only possible to reply in the negative: not writing exposes all the nerves, so we write.

In *The Wall,* a novel by Marlen Haushofer, a woman spends several days on vacation in a mountain chalet. One morning, she wakes to discover that an accident has taken place during the night: quite inexplicably, an invisible wall has fallen, separating her from the rest of the world, which has been completely annihilated.

The novel takes the form of a diary, which begins: "I'm not writing for the sheer joy of writing; so many things have happened to me that I must write if I am not to lose my reason. There's no one here to think and care for me. . . . I've taken on this task to keep me from staring into the gloom and being frightened."

Although it might seem like a work of science fiction, there is nothing unrecognizable about the world of *The Wall.* We know solitude; we are familiar with our attempts to face up to it.

We build houses, we plant gardens, we give birth to children, we learn new words in foreign languages, we climb mountains, we surf waves, we learn to dance or bake cakes, we strip down, we rub up against love. Some of us hurl ourselves into our lives, seizing hold of it, while others stand aside: they are writing it.

What a strange way of being in the world, this retreat to a lookout point. We are life's attendees, close enough to it to grasp its nuances, but maintaining a distance from its noise as from its certainties, so they cannot prejudice the blank page. We can still sketch out maps, pretend as if we know where we're going, but writing is a path without a destination; writing has the unsettling beauty of that which leads nowhere, sometimes for months on end.

Writing is a nationless gesture, an unmooring, an escape into unknown territories. My novels take me for a ride, lead me astray. I think I'm moving forward. After several weeks of writing, all I can say for sure is that my route has led straight into an impasse. The narrative gets away from me; it waits, elsewhere.

I can't avoid veering off-course like this. Giving in to getting lost is a necessary step in the process. Giving in to losing, too. Admitting to having been vanquished, beaten. Accepting that I have to give up any attempt to win out over writing and to abandon everything I thought I knew for sure. You have to move forward in the dark, feeling your way, stumbling over the words that suddenly stop short, the paragraphs that balk. Language is not an inanimate object to be taken up and bent to our will—*it* transforms *us,* whether we are readers or writers.

It tries to lay hold of what flickers in the recesses of our memories, landscapes, silhouettes; it detains us, it catches up to us when we think we no longer believe in it—words are there, tangible, alive. Why do we write? Though I've forgotten how Joyce Carol Oates's *Foxfire: Confessions of a Girl Gang* ends, I know the following lines by heart:

Whatever you do, with whom you do it or whether you do it alone, and when, and how, and why, to what mysterious end—it's balanced against nothing, against Death and forgetting. *You* balanced against oblivion.

I grew up in Ceaușescu's Romania.

When I arrived in Paris at the age of twelve, Nadia Comăneci's worldwide fame had temporarily put the country in the limelight, but for the young French people I met, the Communist countries remained a monolithic "bloc," sad and gray, without nuance; a fictive world. Where the spies and prostitutes always come from in the movies—*Eastern Europe.*

The words we used did not hold the same meaning.

For the students in my seventh-grade class, a passport meant excitement, vacations abroad. The Romanians, however, muttered the word; it had all the dangerous seduction of a secret. *Pașaportul.* No one had one because no one was allowed to leave the country, apart from a few very privileged cases.

For the French kids, doing the shopping at Monoprix was a chore. For me, it was a treat. I explored every aisle, amazed by the abundance of things to buy, beautiful, brightly colored things.

My classmates in junior high were irritated by the commercials at the cinema; I didn't dare admit how passionately I loved their gauzy world, where women had odor-free azure periods and fluttered their eyelids as they enjoyed a yogurt in slow motion.

For them, having one's phone tapped was something from a spy film; for me, it was a memory: when we picked up the receiver in Bucharest, a strange static indicated there was someone else on the line; I even sometimes heard the agents making jokes. The other students snorted when I told them. *My* parents had had their phones tapped? What a liar!

I declined to explain the daily paranoia that was life in Romania under Ceaușescu. A world in which we never knew who was who—informer or friend or both at once?

Since I couldn't seem to make any friends, I started writing down the things I couldn't share. My anecdotes, which they called nonsense, were the raw material for my fiction. One morning, a girl at a neighboring desk spotted a sheet of typewritten paper sticking out of my notebook. A story? Could she read it? At recreation, she came to find me. So what happened next?

The door had cracked open.

Every day, after school, I worked on what happened next. Next was the French officials who got it into their heads that my parents, a simple pair of literature teachers, were spying for the Romanians.

Next was the story of Irina, who had fled, smuggled over the border hidden in the trunk of a diplomat's car.

Next was the story of my father's friend, a poet who was imprisoned in the 1960s for "subversion," who every morning was made to believe by his jailers that today was the day he would be executed.

Next was the story of Maria Vecerdea, whom I loved like my own grandmother, whom I knew, when we left Romania, that I would never see again.

Perhaps we begin writing to provide a "what happened next" for the things we've lost, to make up a story for what no longer is. To place a little red pin on a map to indicate that we are *here,* we are alive. Memories may wither, but words remain intact; they are our geography of time.

My classmates were right: writing is so much *nonsense,* on the margins of reality, at a remove from the truth, because it doesn't exist. And this precious nonsense connects us to each other, writers to readers, like a solemn pledge, a contract with just one stipulation: that we will believe one another.

We are the children of the novels we have loved; they nestle in the crook of all we have lost, all we lack; they hold everything that escapes our grasp, which passes us by too quickly to be understood. We are made of stories that don't belong to us; they irrigate us and haunt us, we who "walk in the night beneath what is written up yonder, equally senseless in our wishes, in our joys, and in our affliction" (Diderot).

Keeping a diary is also a kind of pledge, a children's game we never give up. A game whose rules we determine: we will tell ourselves our own story, as if to someone else.

We will reveal ourselves without pretenses; we will unveil our hidden faces. We will confess everything, at once our own subject and object, writing ourselves in all our stubbornness and anger, our hesitation and determination. And as we write, a new self will emerge.

To keep a diary, regularly or sporadically, is a commitment. To say *I* is to assert our singularity.

Anne Frank's *I* reflects everything that belongs to us, that she has lost: the light of day, the breeze, the blinding sun and the infinite darkness of what we can't perceive, out there between the stars. It contains a little bit of everything and nothing: everyday life in the Annex was also a series of dinners to be prepared, coffee to be warmed up, books with dog-eared pages, arguments and tears, and even, defying the opacity of the blacked-out windows, a tiny corner of sky, up in the attic.

Anne Frank's *I* is addictive. We want more, again. We follow her little *I* through so many contradictory emotions, as she declares she doesn't love her mother and feels so alone she bursts into tears. An *I* that could be maliciously droll, with no scruples whatsoever about settling scores with the people around her. An *I* that knows, at the age of fourteen, that politics is not a subject for grown-ups, but an intolerable daily life for children.

An *I* that doesn't have time to waste trying to be "appropriate." Putting aside false modesty, Anne Frank meticulously describes her vagina, masturbation, and her panic attacks.

An *I* that fights, as well; that refuses to obey the limits imposed on her by Fritz Pfeffer, the grown-up with whom she shares her bedroom. He monopolizes their little table, saying, sarcastically, but what could she possibly have to do that is so important? What is this "work" on which Anne spends so much of her time? A knitting manual, perhaps? She stands up to him, defends her meager territory, argues her case. She needs these two afternoons a week when she can write uninterruptedly. He takes offense; he's never heard of such egotism. He, a grown man, is expected to give up his place to a little kid and her diary? How could she have more to say than he, cooped up for the same reasons, with no life left to live?

How wrong he is, this grown man.

The family is a microcosm, ruled by the same conflicts and thirst for power as any other society.

They say of women who write about their experiences that they are writing about *themselves,* that their narratives are *personal.* A man's journal, however, is thought to contain universal truths. The task of writing the world has long been the preserve of those who can journey out into it, the travelogues of the great voyageurs. The examination of feelings was left to women; they were assigned an understanding of intimate matters, of interior, domestic, or sexual concerns.

Anne Frank's world extends as far out as possible; she plumbed its depths, she scaled its heights. She defies her imprisonment, her *I* knocks into its walls. She furiously hurls herself against its limitations: there is no question that her life will be different from her mother's and "all the women who go about their work and are then forgotten." She defies identity, a German immigrant while also passionately Dutch. No sooner does she affirm something than she cancels it with a *why;* no sooner has she written *I* than she writes *we;* no sooner is she twelve than she's fifteen—barely a teenager, she won't live to become a woman.

She'll sleep later, there's too much to learn. She hungers for knowledge, reading, at random, a biography of Galileo or Charles V, histories of the Seven Years' War, the Nine Years' War, magazines about film stars, genealogies of the European royal families, Anton Springer's history of art, young adult novels, the stories of Theseus, Oedipus, Orpheus. There is also much to learn about the world outside, which forbids her existence, which turns her future into nothingness. What does Anne Frank not talk about?

It is nearly eleven o'clock; I still haven't left Otto and Edith and Margot Franks' bedroom. Perched on the camp bed, I read over my notes. For a moment I think about sending a text message or calling someone. The prospect of having to answer their questions dissuades me. "So? How are you finding it?" they will ask.

Because I'd have to admit that I really don't know. I don't know how I'm finding it.

To find out how I'm finding it, I would have to tell myself a story, I would have to write it. The present moment, which I am not writing, floats, a formless rough draft. It is by writing what I'm experiencing that I understand what I'm experiencing.

Since I began this project, I've been warned three times. The director of the museum mentioned that there were some people who had been devoured by the story of Anne Frank. Laureen Nussbaum cautioned me: we can't content ourselves with reading only what suits us in the *Diary.* And the night guard of the Annex had also advised me that it was easy to get lost there.

People who build labyrinths will tell you: if you want to get out, you must avoid the center.

"The center is not a point. / Otherwise it would be easy to reach it. / It is not even the distillation of a point to its infinity. / The center is the absence / of a point, of infinity, and even of absence / and can only be reached through absence," writes Roberto Juarroz in his collection *Vertical Poetry.*

* * *

Where is the heart of the museum? Is it this teenager's bedroom—nothing but a cubbyhole—to which thousands of visitors flock each year, or are we simply left with words, time and time again?

The red and white checkered notebook is there, not far from where I sit, in a room in the contemporary museum, under glass like a sacred relic, protected by several highly sophisticated security systems.

Only Teresien da Silva has been authorized to touch it, wearing gloves and in the presence of several other people, including the historian David Barnouw of the Institute for War, Holocaust, and Genocide Studies.

Anne Frank's words are precious—but who owns them?

On August 4, 1944, the Gestapo invades the Annex and completely sacks the place—leaving loose sheets of paper and notebooks strewn on the floor.

The very next day, Miep Gies rushes to gather it all up. She knows how important Anne's diary was to her; she saw her write in it every day. She tucks it all away in a drawer, vowing to return it to Anne when she comes back.

In her autobiography, Miep admits that if she had opened even one of the notebooks, she would have burned them all, because they put her in danger: her name, like those of the other benefactors, appeared in them.

In the summer of 1945, Otto Frank receives the letter that confirms the death of his two daughters. Miep resigns herself to giving Anne Frank's writing to her father.

"Here is what your daughter left you."

For months, he can't manage to read any of it. He swore to Anne not to read it without her consent. Would it be a betrayal, or is it, rather, an obligation that his daughter has left him?

When he finally manages to open the notebook, each of her sentences shakes him to his core. Anne's voice only deepens the void created by her absence. He reads passages aloud to Miep, to Laureen Nussbaum's parents; he talks only of her, and in the present tense: do you know what Anne says, what Anne thinks?

Every Sunday, he goes to see other survivors; though they don't speak about what they've lived through, they do exchange the bits of information they've managed to discover. They are all looking for loved ones, not knowing if they're alive or dead.

Otto has no one left to worry about. What he does have he carries with him everywhere: his daughter's writing, her words that must be shared. So no one will ever have to tell such a story again.

Otto proposes reading an excerpt to the other survivors. One, struck by Otto's daughter's writerly voice, asks if he can borrow the notebook. Otto hesitates. But he does know one thing: his daughter dreamed of being read.

This first reader is deeply impressed and shares the notebook with a friend, a history professor, who is in turn deeply moved. Why not send the text to a publisher? Though Otto Frank is initially reticent, once again, he chooses to be faithful to his daughter's dreams.

But what sense would a publisher be able to make of this mess of papers, some of which are so alike as to be easily confused; Anne split up the red and white notebook into two versions of the diary. Then there are two accounting books, a chemistry exercise book belonging to Margot, over two hundred loose sheets, not to mention the short stories and the notebook into which Anne Frank copied noteworthy passages from her reading.

If, for Teresien da Silva, Otto Frank was a man faced with extraordinary choices, this was certainly one of them. He devoted himself to continuing his daughter's work, spending all his time on it, minutely comparing variants, working line by line. What would *she* have wanted? What would *she* have chosen?

Otto Frank didn't *decide* which passages to keep; he had to choose between them—there's a difference, Laureen Nussbaum told me during our meeting. He was not a literary man. And his choices bear this out: in order to create a linear narrative, Otto Frank blends pages from the "raw" diary with those which Anne had revised.

But didn't he censor his daughter? Not at all, Laureen says vehemently when I ask her, and he didn't touch her stylistic choices, either. It was Anne herself who deleted passages she thought were too personal, thinking they wouldn't be of interest to her future readers.

In 1947, a small Dutch publisher agreed to publish the diary, on the condition that Otto Frank cut the passages in which his daughter unambiguously mentions her sexuality and her period.

As for the German editors, they chose to restore those passages but required certain "negative passages" concerning Nazi anti-Semitism be deleted: such passages might "offend" readers.

No edition, in any country, mentions the work of revising that Anne Frank undertook herself. The *Diary* is presented as if it had been spontaneously composed by a teenager. The first American edition chose for its cover a picture of Anne at the age of ten, three years before she began writing. Its author's precociousness became the work's main selling point.

Laureen Nussbaum is one of the first academics to have analyzed the *Diary* as a work of literature. One of her articles is called "Is Anne Frank at last taken seriously as a writer?"

Who does Anne Frank belong to, asks Cynthia Ozick in an essay for the *New Yorker* in 1997. Who does the *Diary* belong to, when reading it has become a rite of passage for millions of adolescents since 1947? To its readers? To its publishers? To her father, thanks to whom it was published?

There is so much love, so very much love around her. A mad love, all-consuming, which gives some people the idea that they can speak on behalf of the girl they love, more loudly than her, in her place.

It's 1951. The American writer Meyer Levin is living in France, having been a foreign correspondent during the war, one of the first to enter Bergen-Belsen camp after the Liberation.

He is floored by the *Diary,* which has just been published in France. He has been waiting for that voice, "the voice from the mass grave," the mass grave he has seen with his own eyes.

He immediately writes to Otto Frank to convey his emotion: it is absolutely imperative that Anne Frank's words be shared far and wide. Although the *Diary* has appeared in France, the Netherlands, and Germany, it has met with only limited success. This extraordinary text has to be translated and published in the United States and adapted for the stage.

Meyer Levin proves particularly persuasive. Despite his reservations, Otto Frank agrees, and Levin begins work on a theatrical adaptation.

He throws himself into his mission with religious fervor. To anyone he meets—editors, journalists, writers—he describes himself, amazed, as having been "chosen" by Anne Frank's father. An American editor is persuaded by his ardor, and the *Diary* is published in June 1952, with a modest print run.

The critics immediately laud the young writer's literary talent. It goes into a second printing, then a third. The book's success attracts theatre producers and famous playwrights like Arthur Miller, Lillian Hellman, and Carson McCullers.

Meanwhile Levin has finished a first draft of his adaptation. He sends it to Otto Frank, who tactfully calls it "faithful" but prefers to seek the editor's advice.

She rejects the text. Levin is furious. He appeals to Otto Frank, begs him to intervene; they had an agreement, didn't they?

Otto Frank protests; he promised nothing, signed nothing with this American writer who has pursued and harassed him, who has latched onto his daughter, brandishing her like a flag for some cause, to the point of making her the subject of a dispute. This he finds unbearable. Let them work it out between themselves, these editors, these producers!

Everyone around Levin urges him to give it up, but he no longer listens to anyone, not his friends or his enemies. He seeks legal advice: he will sue Otto Frank! He'll sue the producer! He will fight for *her.*

Everyone around Otto Frank is worried: he has been seriously ill, he needs to be left in peace. If Levin goes on like this, he will end up killing Anne's father.

In the summer of 1953, the project has stalled. It's gone through several different writers, and the producer has been replaced by a tried-and-true Broadway hitmaker called Kermit Bloomgarden. For him, a good show should never be "demoralizing."

His verdict comes down swiftly: the story of Anne Frank is "too Jewish" and "much too sad" for the American public to take any interest. They're going to need a new adaptation of the *Diary*, something more "lighthearted." To write the script he turns to a pair of writers with an unimpeachable resumé, specializing in feel-good movies: their work included *Easter Parade* and *Father of the Bride.*

They promise a show that will feature "some nice comedic moments emerging from a tragic situation."

The director chosen by the producers, Garson Kanin, is famous for upbeat comedies, like *Born Yesterday.* Kanin agrees with the playwrights and the producer: the show should be neither "too Jewish" nor "too sad."

If Anne Frank is no longer Jewish, then any of us could be Anne Frank. The *Diary* could and should become a book with universal relevance. Everyone sets about doing just this.

A paragraph, for instance, from April 11, 1944, has to go: "We're Jews in chains. . . . Who has inflicted this on us? Who has set us apart from all the rest? Who has put us through such suffering?" Kanin is convinced that "without this special pleading . . . the play has an opportunity to spread its theme into the infinite." It is accordingly cut and replaced with this passage: "We're not the only people that've had to suffer. There've always been people that've had to . . . sometimes one race . . . sometimes another." The brief reflection on Hanukkah is cut as well. No German in uniform appears onstage. And, finally, the romance between Anne and Peter takes center stage, as it must in all successful family entertainment.

Levin gets wind of these rewrites. They're turning the *Diary* into sentimental nonsense! And it is such recent history—how dare they? Persuaded that he will win out in the end, he continues to perfect "his" version.

Literary New York turns its back on him, calling him paranoid, depressed, possessed, haunted, ridiculous. No doubt he is. And perhaps he also suffers from survivor's guilt, as his wife, Tereska Torrès, writes in her book about these events, *The Haunted Houses of Meyer Levin.*

Perhaps Levin is haunted by what he saw at Bergen-Belsen, "the hair of dead girls, all the little girls, and the shoes of dead children, and the prayer shawls and the dented bowls, the wooden bedframes and the filthy straw on which Anne Frank closed her eyes and let her spirit slip away."

We have to do something, Levin says to his lawyers. Anne Frank's words, her *real* words, have to be heard on stage. They won't be if this goes ahead.

A few days before opening night, a journalist from the *New York Times* praises the play, based "partly" on the story of eight Jews hiding from the Nazis. "Mostly, though, it is the story of one of them—a young girl who refused to be robbed of the adventure of adolescence."

Otto Frank does not attend the premiere. He will never see the play staged.

In an interview, Kanin would claim his play "[had] mainly to do with human courage, faith, hope, brotherhood, love, and self-sacrifice."

The *Herald Tribune* would write that the play avoided "hating the Nazis, hating what they did to millions of innocent people," and was instead "glowing, moving, frequently humorous. . . . It is not grim."

The story has been purged of anything that might offend or anger, but that is not enough for the U.S. State Department, which, in 1956, refuses to send the show to the international theatre festival in Paris, despite its success—French officials worry that a show "based on the persecution of the Jews might endanger cordial relations with Germany."

Who owns Anne Frank? Her father, who after reading her diary admitted that he hadn't really known his daughter? Meyer Levin, obsessed by the need to allow her voice to be heard, to such an extent that he drowned it out? The theatre producers, whose efforts to replace her voice with another, less "sad" and more "universal," were rewarded with a Pulitzer Prize?

In 1958, it is Hollywood's turn to claim a piece of Anne Frank. An unknown young woman, an Audrey Hepburn–like model, will play Anne. Millie Perkins has never acted before. Interviewed at Cannes, she says she was amazed at having been chosen out of ten thousand young girls. Had she heard of Anne Frank before the audition? Not really, no, she murmurs, prettily lowering her eyes, her fake lashes brushing her cheeks. But before filming began, she read it, of course. The *Diary*? No, Millie Perkins answers. The play.

George Stevens, the director, was a lieutenant-colonel in the Army Signal Corps who filmed the liberation of Dachau.

Perhaps this is why he is so determined to tell Anne's whole story. He plans to end the film on a wide shot of the young girl, dressed in a prisoner's uniform, in the fog of the concentration camp.

A few weeks before the film is released, 20th Century Fox holds test screenings, at which audiences complain the ending is "too sad" and the story really "too hard."

The producers ask Stevens to film a different ending; it would be better to end on "a hopeful note" so that audiences might be more able to "identify."

The camera sweeps over the terrified faces of the eight people in hiding. Harsh voices are getting closer: the Gestapo, come to arrest them. The Germans rap on the Annex door. "Otto Frank" gets up, takes a travel bag, which he hands to "Margot," then another, which he gives to his wife, and a last one, which he gives to his younger daughter. He sits back down, as if reassured, and in a reflective tone he says, while the Nazis encircle them, "For the past two years we have lived in fear. Now we can live in hope."

Cut.

The ecstatic face of Millie Perkins/Anne Frank appears superimposed over a vast sky filled with fluffy clouds; graceful birds soar here and there. In voiceover:

"In spite of everything I still believe that people are really good at heart."

THE END.

The trailer for the film promises: "No greater suspense story has ever been told than 20th Century Fox's masterful production of the *Diary of Anne Frank*! Here is the thrill of her first kiss! Here is the wonder of her youth! The excitement of her first love! The miracle of her laughter!"

The film, which came out in 1959, would win four Oscars and worldwide distribution.

This fictional Anne, full of sweetness and hope, triumphs over Anne Frank, sending her back to her shadowy Annex.

If we are all Anne Frank, there is no more Anne Frank.

In *Le Moi des demoiselles,* Philippe Lejeune, whose research focuses on autobiography and the diary, says this of nineteenth-century diary keepers: "We teach young girls resignation. They wait, keeping busy, and filling up their diaries with their woes; the diary is a prison within a prison, a flight to the interior, a message in a bottle."

Anne Frank threw her bottle into the sea, and we found it. We have treasured it, astounded that it reached us. She is so precious to us that we are more interested in the bottle than what it contained.

In the weeks before I traveled to Amsterdam, whenever I mentioned the trip, my friends exhorted me not to make my book "too sad," because Anne Frank is "life itself." Some remember the budding love story with Peter, others her savage descriptions of Fritz Pfeffer, her fights with her mother, and the way she claimed to be a "terrible flirt." They were all right. The *Diary* is full of love, and tears, and arguments over nothing, so many noses thumbed at Evil. Anne Frank was funny, frivolous, immature, despite all the rest. The rest that she couldn't write down.

The diary comes to a close on the entry of August 1st, and it is tempting to close it with her, on her.

Societies form around narratives that they deem important to transmit. The most famous quote from the *Diary,* written on July 15, 1944, is this one: "I still believe, in spite of everything, that people are truly good at heart."

This phrase is followed by another, a few lines later, which is never quoted:

> It's utterly impossible for me to build my life on a foundation of chaos, suffering and death. I see the world being slowly transformed into a wilderness, I hear the approaching thunder that, one day, will destroy us too, I feel the suffering of millions. And yet, when I look up at the sky, I somehow feel that everything will change for the better, that this cruelty too shall end, that peace and tranquility will return once more.

What we choose to quote from the texts we revere indicates what we would like to take from them. While we very much want Anne Frank to speak to us about people being "truly good at heart," it is unsurprising that the following passage, written on May 3, 1944, is hardly ever cited, either:

> I don't believe the war is simply the work of politicians and capitalists. Oh no, the common man is every bit as guilty; otherwise, people and nations would have rebelled long ago! There's a destructive urge in people, the urge to rage, murder and kill. And until all of humanity, without exception, undergoes a metamorphosis, wars will continue to be waged, and everything that has been carefully built up, cultivated and grown will be cut down and destroyed, only to start all over again!

What a strange Hollywood humanism, this preference we have for thinking of people as being "truly good at heart." What a cruel optimism, that in the name of "hope," we prefer to forget this passage, written on Friday, May 26, 1944: "What will we do if we're ever . . . no, I mustn't write that down. But the question won't let itself be pushed to the back of my mind today; on the contrary, all the fear I've ever felt is looming before me in all its horror."

Anne Frank doesn't allow herself to finish her sentence. Perhaps it is our duty to do so on her behalf.

On August 4, 1944, the Gestapo enters the Annex.

The Franks are detained four days at the headquarters of the Gestapo, who then transfer them to the holding camp at Westerbork.

Otto Frank's daughters are assigned grueling work taking apart old batteries. They work for sixteen hours a day.

The Allies have landed in France, the Germans are going to lose the war, everyone thinks they'll stop deporting Jews. But why would they stop?

They go on deporting Jews.

At dawn on September 3, 1944, a single train leaves Westerbork, the last convoy headed to Auschwitz-Birkenau, containing 1,900 men, women, and children, including the eight occupants of the Annex, whom the SS stuff into cattle cars, seventy per car. There they will stay for three days and two nights, in the dark, with nothing to eat or drink, and nowhere to relieve themselves. No one knows which direction the train is going, or how long the journey will last.

On September 5th, the train stops.

We have to imagine but we can't imagine the blinding floodlights, the howling dogs, the barking SS officers, how to imagine what it feels like to be separated, in the space of a few seconds, from your wife, your husband, your children, being whipped and bludgeoned. We know that those who were too young, weak, or old were separated from the group.

On September 6th, the Nazis push all the children under the age of five into the gas chambers, as well as 549 adults.

The Franks, the Van Pels, and Fritz Pfeffer are sent to forced labor.

The SS orders them to strip down, shaves them, tattoos their left arms. They no longer have first or last names, only numbers. Anne and Margot are placed in barracks usually reserved for prisoners with scabies. Between October 20th and 28th, more than six thousand people, including a thousand people younger than eighteen, are gassed less than two hours after their arrival.

On October 28th (though other sources give the date as November 1st) Anne and Margot Frank are separated from their mother. They will never see her again.

Once more they are stuffed into a cattle car.

No one among the three hundred women knows they are being taken to a German camp called Bergen-Belsen. Some will die during the trip, which lasts three days and three nights.

When they arrive, they are made to walk six kilometers.

The camp is overcrowded, with neither privies nor lighting. Everywhere there are stacks of cadavers, naked and covered with snow. The bodies of the living are packed into tents. Anne and Margot Frank inherit the worst spots of all: a bunk exposed to the glacial wind.

The final days of the Frank sisters have been told in fragments by survivors who remember having encountered them. Everyone mentions Anne's voice, Margot's voice, begging someone to close the tent, that they're so cold. Everyone says they heard them die, their voices diminish.

Anne and Margot Frank, skeletal, scabies-ridden, lice-infested, die of hunger, of cold, and of typhus.

Margot succumbs first. We don't know the exact date of Anne's death, which was officially recorded as March 31, 1945.

While her short life has been documented to the point of obsession, her death consigned her to the same fate as all the other victims of the Holocaust: Anne Frank has no tomb. Her body rests somewhere in a mass grave, like the other fifty thousand people who died in Bergen-Belsen. Until 1999, there wasn't even a headstone with her name on it.

How beloved she is, this young Jewish girl who is no longer. The most famous Holocaust victim in the world. The Holocaust victim whose diary is the most read in the world, even if it's missing the ending.

Maybe that's why she is so loved. If she had survived, we know what she would have told us, what she would have written: Westerbork Auschwitz-Birkenau Bergen-Belsen.

Maybe we wouldn't have wanted to read it.

The final entry in her diary is dotted with ellipses, like so many silences, those of a little girl who's been locked up, of a "prisoner in a cage," as Cynthia Ozick puts it.

> "If all men are good, there can be no Auschwitz."
>
> *Bruno Bettelheim, survivor of Dachau and Buchenwald*

On the day after my night in the Annex, Ronald Leopold wants to introduce me to Rosetta, nicknamed Ted, who is ninety-five years old. She pours us some tea, insists I help myself to another biscuit. Ted is bright and lively, she loves painting and flowers, and she is delighted with her new tablet. She is excited to be going to Paris in the autumn to see an exhibition.

She was fifteen when she was arrested. She was deported to Bergen-Belsen.

She speaks with her face turned away from us, as if she were carrying out an obligation. We can't say we didn't know.

Her hands take the form of air quotes. "At Bergen-Belsen, our 'living' conditions . . ."

She breaks off. Different words are needed.

Or perhaps no words at all.

She lets go of words, they yield to her breathing, a labored breathing.

> "The conditions of . . .   our . . .   survival . . .   in Bergen-Belsen . . .   were . . ."
> *[Breathing]*

A few weeks later, she sends me an email: "I could tell you a thousand times about the inhumanity, the nightmare that was Bergen-Belsen, but it would be useless. You would never be able to imagine it. Just as well."

To admit that we can't imagine something, that we mustn't imagine something—how can we pretend to imagine something?—is not a failure of writing. That verb *to imagine* has no place in my night. However, we have to try anyway, even and especially if we can't manage it. We have to try to imagine.

It's almost midnight and I still haven't gone into Anne Frank's room, even though it's right next door. I'll go in later.

I walk. I go from one room to the next, as if I have to be somewhere, but where? I go up and down the stairs, full of nervous energy, waiting for fatigue to come over me. I open my computer, reread my notes, check my email. The flashlight on my telephone sweeps over the faded ochre wallpaper in the Van Pels' bedroom, the enamel washbasin protected by a red and white ribbon.

I rush back downstairs, return to "my" room. I have inspected every inch of it, modest as it is: a Dickens novel, which belonged to Otto, who was trying to improve his English, Edith's prayerbook, and a folded sheet of paper with corrections in red ink—Margot's Latin coursework.

The door to *her* room is half open. I would like to say that I went in, that I was able to be reflective there, that a great calmness came over me, that I cried.

But something is there, something diffuse, which keeps me from doing any of it, something unnameable. I berate myself, distressed that the night is having this effect on me; what happened to being pragmatic? This "something" is neither a ghost nor a presence. It's a sensation of overfullness, as if it were impossible to find a place for myself in that room.

I hesitate for a few moments in the doorway. In the half-dark, the pictures pinned to the wall conjure up the teenager who put them there: the faces of Hollywood actresses, reproductions of famous paintings, pictures of children cut out of women's magazines, postcards.

It was Otto Frank who thought Anne should take her treasures with her when they went into hiding. "Thanks to Father—who brought my entire postcard and movie-star collection here beforehand—and to a brush and a pot of glue, I was able to plaster the walls with pictures," she wrote on July 11, 1942.

The clock strikes midnight.

Then I remember the exhibition about these images in the contemporary part of the building. But how to get back there from the Annex?

The walkie-talkie coughs out a few words in Dutch and then a woman's voice asking, "It's not too cold up there, is it?"

Well, I've got nothing to complain about, I tell her, not *here.*

A few minutes later, Gladys, the night guard, appears at the door of the Annex and offers me a felted wool blanket. She reminds me of the rules: no eating, drinking, or taking photographs. That said, she doesn't mind if I do, as long as I'm careful, and she points to the thermos sticking out of my bag.

She gives me a look full of sympathy: surely I don't need to put myself through this to write? I reassure her: I chose to come here, no one is forcing me to do anything, all is well.

I can't manage to go in Anne Frank's bedroom, but that I don't tell her.

"Do you mind if I stay here a moment?" she asks. Sitting side by side on the camp bed, we get to know each other.

Gladys tells me about a pair of actors who were preparing to play Otto and Anne in a film. They requested permission to spend the night here, to "soak up the atmosphere." But in the end, they called her at one o'clock in the morning, feeling ill at ease, and left.

If you make it through the night, you'll have been the first to have done it, she concludes, as if she were encouraging me to beat some record, but for doing what?

We're whispering. It's funny, isn't it? As if we were afraid of disturbing someone. No matter how many years she's worked there, Gladys still sometimes feels as if she ought to knock before entering the Annex. It's an apartment, that's why, but, after all . . . It's not a church, she adds.

And what had I felt, when I'd gone into her room? Did I feel pensive? Some visitors had wanted to leave flowers, as if before an altar. They leave stuffed animals, their own diaries . . .

I give in and pretend that I have gone into the bedroom, and by the way perhaps she might be able to guide me to the exhibition about what Anne had on her walls? Gladys spares me the trouble of explaining why I want to see the enlarged reproductions of the photos when the originals are right next door, so close to where we sit.

We pass through a series of corridors and then Gladys stops before an unremarkable beige door: through here, we can move back and forth between the Annex and the contemporary museum without following the tourists' path. It's a shortcut, a secret within a secret. To remember this unmarked door, Gladys advises me to remember a detail in the room.

In a glass case are two official documents in German and a portrait of Margot Frank, with the serious smile of an anxious young girl. Margot's name appears on one of the documents: it's a list that the headmistress of her school drew up for the Nazis on July 16, 1941. "It is my honor to present you with this list containing the names of students with Jewish blood."

Margot will be the one to show me the way, the silent one, the girl whose words have been lost.

The large rooms of the contemporary museum by night are calming. This is a more appropriate role for me, that of an everyday visitor.

The exhibition takes up several panels. Anne Frank's postcards are annotated; I read the explanatory captions, I take notes, I take photographs of photographs.

At this point in the night, I am not yet aware that it will be impossible for me to face the *real* postcards in the *real* bedroom. I haven't yet realized that I prefer the fiction of an organized exhibition, the narrative over the reality.

Children are afraid of the dark, of being alone, of ghosts and of monsters. At the cinema, they cover their eyes with their hands while peeking between their fingers, to get a glimpse of what they fear.

As we grow up, we lose our courage, we look away. We move on to something else.

I walk quickly past an array of pictures of Anne Frank, a variety of different facial expressions.

In May 1935, she is an unwilling subject: pouting, she turns away from the lens, her Peter Pan collar showing under her wool cardigan. In May 1937 she's impatient, she doesn't have the time to sit still; the blurriness of the image proves it. In May 1941, her final year of freedom, her puffed-sleeve dress makes her look like a little girl, which she's not. In her pale face we see the trace of something far away.

May 1942: the image is trying not to write History, in the hope that *all of this* will just be a shameful episode, to be forgotten. The frame tightens around Anne Frank. In this photograph we don't see it, but we know: the young girl's dress has been branded with a yellow star.

Diane Arbus said of her photographs that they were "a secret about a secret," offering "the proof that something was there and no longer is. Like a stain. And the stillness of them is boggling. You can turn away but when you come back they'll still be there looking at you."

I turn away from the pictures but Anne Frank is still there, staring at me. The muted lighting of the museum reveals her more than a brighter light would: a close-up of her face takes up an entire wall, with no date, and no caption.

The past is a flash, a moment, it no longer exists. Anne Frank is just like every other teenager, suddenly blushing without knowing why; it may be that we're embarrassing them with all our questions, our comments. Maybe we shouldn't go into their bedrooms.

I walked toward her. And I saw something I'd never noticed, a detail, no doubt meaningless. Something that hadn't made it into History, though we know everything about her.

On Anne Frank's downy cheeks, there are little spots here and there, forming a childish pattern.

Anne Frank had freckles.

I am so close to her that I no longer see Anne Frank, but a person called Anne. I stay there, face to face with her, for a long time. Everything is too big. The museum is too big, the photo is too big, the night is too long and desolate. She is so alone and so small, one single syllable, Anne.

* * *

Anne the teenager, such a teenager, impatiently waiting, every week, for Victor, one of their protectors, to bring her *Cinema & Theater*, a magazine that celebrated the art of performance but also the Nazi regime.

Such a teenager that she collected photographs of actresses with powdered skin, drawn-on eyebrows, and outlandishly long eyelashes. A puny, pale teenager condemned to a world without sunlight, who pinned on her bedroom wall images of a blindingly bright world, a world lit to its best angle, glitzy and glittering. A world of healthy bodies, firmed through massage and care, bodies trained for glory, like that of Sonja Henie, the figure skater.

Sonja presides over Anne's bedroom walls, an imposing figure, an ice virgin in a white tutu, hair pulled back in an ermine headband. There she reigns, perched on the backseat of a white automobile, staring at the camera, her immaculate dress spread out on the leather seats.

What is it about her that so bewitched Anne Frank? Her precocity? At only fourteen years old, the three-time Olympic champion had revolutionized figure skating with her decision to wear a short skirt and white skates, instead of the long skirts of the period and the traditional black skates.

Did Anne Frank know that Sonja Henie was presented to Hitler at the 1936 Olympic Games? She gave quite the performance, saluting him with grace and humility—genuflecting, curtseying—and then, her arm dead straight, wearing a form-fitting satin dress the color of cream, she cried out with force and conviction: "Heil Hitler!"

Sonja would doubtless not have appreciated that Anne chose to pin her up beside the Chinese-American actress Anna May Wong.

Throughout her career, she was forever consigned to the role of the understudy. She kept running up against the Motion

Picture Production Code, which outlawed "intimate" scenes between actors of different races. Anna May Wong had to settle for teaching the white actresses chosen to play Asian roles how to correctly hold their chopsticks.

The place of honor is reserved for Greta Garbo: above the collaborationist ice-skater. Garbo, a beautiful woman and as desirable as a young man, whom producers called "the recluse" because she refused to play along with the game of parties and film promotion.

Anne Frank glued a photo of Deanna Durbin above her bed, and maybe, before she went into hiding, she would have been able to see one of her films. Deanna Durbin, the child star of optimistic, saccharine comedies whose names have been utterly forgotten: *Three Smart Girls, Three Smart Girls Grow Up, Lady On a Train.*

Mussolini wrote Deanna an open letter, published in *Il Popolo d'Italia,* begging her to do something, to convince Roosevelt not to enter the war.

Anne loved the women's magazine *Libelle:* she cut out filmy photographs of little girls, their light hair in curls, wearing smock dresses. Children with milky complexions, playing at hoop rolling in the luxuriant countryside. Anne would never see nature again.

In her bedroom, Anne Frank pinned up propaganda images of a blond, triumphantly Aryan world, in which she was but a stain to be erased, a cancer to eradicate.

"One day this terrible war will be over. The time will come when we'll be people again and not just Jews!" wrote Anne Frank in her diary on April 11, 1944.

To this wish, never to be granted, Philip Roth replied in *The Ghostwriter:*

> Once a year the Franks sang a harmless Chanukah song, said some Hebrew words, lighted some candles, exchanged some presents. . . . It took nothing—that was the horror. And that was the truth. . . . The Franks could gather together by the radio to listen to concerts of Mozart, Brahms, and Beethoven; they could entertain themselves with Goethe and Dickens and Schiller; she could look night after night through the genealogical tables of all of Europe's royal families for suitable mates for Princess Elizabeth and Princess Margaret Rose; she could write passionately in her diary of her love for Queen Wilhelmina and her desire for Holland to be her fatherland—and none of it made any difference. Europe was not theirs nor were they Europe's. . . . Instead, three flights up from a pretty Amsterdam canal, they lived crammed into a hundred square feet with the Van Daans, as isolated and despised as any ghetto Jews. First expulsion, next confinement, and then, in cattle cars and camps and ovens, obliteration. And why? Because the Jewish problem to be solved, the degenerates whose contamination civilized people could no longer abide, were they themselves, Otto and Edith Frank, and their daughters, Margot and Anne.

Without thinking I press the call button on the walkie-talkie. Gladys answers right away: have I finished?

In the video control room, I am a blurry outline of a person, with a calm, composed face, wearing a black skirt and a white blouse, standing before a wall of images.

I don't know what I asked her but no doubt Gladys understood that it was a pretext to hear a voice amid all this silence.

We talk about Jesus, the young man with closed eyes agonizing in his mother's arms: a reproduction of Michelangelo's *Pietà*, which Anne Frank cut out of Springer's *History of Art*, which her father had given her for her birthday. We talk about Otto Frank, who on his return from Auschwitz spent long hours in his daughter's bedroom, trying to cut out the constellation of film stars without tearing the photographs. To keep them near him, to protect them. So no one could harm his daughter's dreams.

We talk about Michelle Obama and the thoughtful message she left in the visitors' book. Gladys told me that every year Queen Beatrix comes to reflect in the room, just as Juliana did before her.

Anne would have been so shocked and happy to have queens visiting her bedroom, murmurs Gladys; it's stupid but that's what I think every time a member of the royal family comes.

The security guard wishes me a good night; someone else will take over for her soon. What about you? she asks. What do you have planned?

The sound has been turned off on the videos in the next room; on the two screens there is playing, on loop, a documentary showing two faces, in a medium shot, speaking silently, subtitled in English.

A white-haired Otto Frank, dressed in a dark suit, is being interviewed by a journalist in the 1970s. He describes how the Gestapo burst into the Annex on August 4, 1944. He describes the way they looked for jewelry and money, rummaging through the armoire in the entryway, Anne's notebooks and loose sheets of paper scattering all over the floor. The subtitles scroll across the screen below Otto Frank's face; when he lowers his eyes, it's as if he were reading them at the same time as I am:

> When Miep returned to the empty Annex, she gathered up all the papers, Anne's notebooks. She didn't read them. She wanted to give them to Anne when she returned. That was not ultimately . . . possible.

To Otto Frank's right, a woman of around seventy wearing a black coat is walking through a wintery landscape, filled with barren trees: this is what remains of Bergen-Belsen. The clipped grass covers a mass grave filled with over ten thousand bodies.

Hannah Goslar was arrested when she was fifteen years old, in 1943, a year before her friend Anne. They had met in primary school; they lived in the same neighborhood, in Merwedeplein. Anne cracked her friends up by dislocating and relocating her shoulder, like a tiny contortionist. Anne, a chatterbox who couldn't stand being contradicted. Hannah's mother would say of her: "God knows everything but Anne knows everything about everything."

Hannah Goslar stops in the middle of the screen, her face frozen:

> In November 1944, I heard that Anne was in the same camp as I was. I sent her a note through the other prisoners. I said I would wait for her at nightfall, by the barbed-wire. During the daytime the Germans would have shot us if they had spotted us there. She walked toward me; I didn't recognize her. I said to her but what are you doing here? I thought you were in Switzerland. It was awful. She was . . .

Then the image and the English subtitles seem to diverge: Hannah smiles as if the pain and anger had been conquered by despair; what comes after grief, nothing that has any meaning, so she smiles, while at the bottom of the screen the words scroll mechanically:

> . . . skeletal, her head shaved, her eyes huge. I was afraid we would be shot; we weren't supposed to be by the barbed-wire. Anne kept saying Mama is dead I'm sure of it and Margot is so sick she's going to die and Papa is surely dead
>
> he was too old   I'm all alone   in the world   I don't have   anyone anymore
>
> I think about it all the time   if Anne had only known   that her father was still alive   she would have held on   you never know   no? If Anne   had only known her father was alive   would she have   lived?
>
> I think of this endlessly   if she had only known   if only she had known   Maybe she would have   you know   there was only a month to go   She had nothing to hold onto   she died a month before the Liberation
>
> If only   but she didn't know.

I turn away from Hannah and leave the room. The speed of my hurried steps makes me ashamed; do the surveillance cameras notice the way I've fled? Is the night guard mocking my lack of courage? I push a door; it opens onto a room that is empty except for a glass case protecting a child's game: the marbles Anne gave to her neighbor before going into hiding; they weren't *essential.*

They are parma pink and coral, they are ochre yellow and jade green, they look as if they've been interrupted mid-game.

One of the marbles, anthracite blue, seems to have escaped wear and tear; it glints and makes me want to pick it up and protect it.

I draw closer; I put my hand on the glass. I don't know how to pray.

I leave behind the museum with its abandoned games, its movie actresses, and its explanatory captions to return to the Annex. It is just after 2 a.m. At 7 I will leave, but I can't without having gone into Anne Frank's bedroom.

Why can't I go in there, what am I doing here, spending this night in the *prison house* of someone who's no longer alive? Maybe my mother was right; she advised me to stick some sleeping pills in my toiletry bag. Maybe 1.5 mg of benzodiazepine will put an end to my questionings.

Lexomil and Temesta were my grandparents' remedy of choice, like everyone else in their circle, immigrant Jews from Russia, Poland, Romania.

They took their sleeping pills every night before bed, though no doctor prescribed them; they shared them around with their friends the moment they showed signs of sadness, the way you'd offer someone some chocolate.

Exile—the loss of one's roots—is a malady whose symptoms are familiar to me. I can describe them not as a sociologist or a psychiatrist might, but as the granddaughter of refugees. I know the disorder experienced by those who have had to change their name, their language, their country, their home, their families, their desires. Survivors and refugees are not heroes. They are people who are exhausted, who are living *as though.* They are as Elie Wiesel described them in *Day:*

> They look like the others. They eat, they laugh, they love. . . . But it isn't true: they are playing, sometimes without even knowing it. Anyone who has seen what they have seen cannot be like the others. . . . A spring snapped inside them from the shock.

They are parents driven mad by the fact that they cannot protect their children. They are parents who beseech their children not to stand out, who teach them the art of disappearing, of blending into the background.

They are grandparents who are wildly proud of their grandchildren's every success, of anything that confirms their belonging to the host country. Grandparents who, upon hearing the recitation of a banal French poem learned in sixth grade, have tears in their eyes.

The summer I was fifteen, I wanted to try out making word-portraits of people, a new exercise for me. I had kept a diary since the age of eight.

My grandfather kindly submitted to my questions.

When was he born? Around 1906. He wasn't sure; they didn't keep strict records in Retchysta, the town where he was born in Belarus.

When did his family flee to Poland from the Russian pogroms? Maybe around 1920; he was a teenager. Where in the Warsaw ghetto did they live? And his sisters? Is it true that one of them was a dentist, that they'd all gone to school, despite the quotas the Poles imposed on the Jews?

He didn't know. He didn't want to think about all that. It didn't matter. It was in the past.

The pages of my notebook remained mostly blank, a minefield of short sentences and question marks.

I ultimately gave up questioning him. He was a man of beginnings, of fresh starts. A being made of hope, who had believed, every time, in the possibility of a normal life.

He hummed all the time. When he did the washing up, when he tidied up his office, at the wheel of his car, while going to bed.

Sometimes I was struck by the thought that he sang like children do, to give themselves courage: a little boy in Retchysta, constantly afraid, in the street, at school, of being singled out, captured, deported. An orphan singing loudly, at the entrance of a too-dark forest, the forest that he chose as the backdrop to all the stories he told me, from which the hero could never escape.

Sometimes, it seemed like he sang so a voice would persist in the darkness.

He was so alone. Without them. On the rare occasions his voice caught, when he stopped humming, his eyes misted. He repeated their names, a litany, a prayer, but to whom? No one heard his prayer:

Sonia Bronia Olga Chava.

His refrain rebounds in the void: these brief, echoing syllables. His sisters, independent young girls, had insisted stubbornly on studying in Warsaw, despite the rules that forbade Jews from sitting near the other students in the amphitheaters, ordering them to sit on designated benches.

Young girls who died in a cattle car carrying them to Auschwitz.

Sonia Bronia Olga Chava.

Like Otto Frank, my grandfather was a victim of *tragic faith* placed in a host country, persuaded that if he made enough of an effort he would be respected and protected. France: a country whose virtues his father had extolled, the land of Victor Hugo and the Declaration of the Rights of Man. He arrived around 1933.

For an immigrant who had nothing, for a hunted man who'd had no choice but to leave everything behind, it didn't take much to abandon the few possessions he had and flee Paris, in search of a place to hide. The French authorities ordered all Jews to wear the yellow star in 1942, and *living* in France became *surviving* France. Although my grandfather was proud of saying that he had immediately understood that he mustn't follow these orders, he never spoke of those who had voted in this anti-Jewish law.

No mention was made of any French responsibility whatsoever.

My grandparents survived by pretending that France really was a haven. They turned forgetting into a form of knowing. They pledged allegiance to amnesia. The everyday remained for them a place of great hostility, in which they dreaded doing the wrong thing, being singled out, treated *like foreigners.* Peace of mind forever eluded them.

Except for Sunday afternoons, when they came together with people who were like them, their Polish, Russian, Romanian friends, members of the same Jewish, secular, Communist organization.

There, for a few hours, they left French the way you remove a too-constricting piece of clothing. They spoke Yiddish or Hebrew. Some knew each other *from before*; they came from the same Russian or Polish village.

Their confidence grew. They were no longer *those immigrants.* They talked animatedly, exchanging views on Georges Marchais's latest television appearance, enthusing over the other guests' taste in music or theatre. They shared ideas about newspaper articles, sang, served cups of boiling hot tea or glasses of vodka, along with strudel and poppyseed cake.

By Monday morning they had changed back into thickly accented foreigners, conscientiously choosing their words, with the caution of people who lack those of the country they live in.

The effort required to be French dominated every day, every moment; the nights at least were a relief, thanks to those little white pills.

To sing someone else's song is a means of paying tribute to them; but it is also to anticipate, or at least to hope, that our version will be superior to theirs.

We approach the microphone, persuaded that our timbre is more suited to the melody, that we will be better able to give voice to our truth than those who have preceded us.

In her study *Children of the Holocaust,* Helen Epstein interviewed the children and grandchildren of Holocaust survivors. Some were told nothing by their parents, but they were haunted nevertheless by a past that was not their own.

When the family tree has been uprooted, the birth of a child takes on a particular importance: the newborn is a proof of survival. He cannot simply exist. He will inherit the duty to live vigorously, for and in place of those who did not survive.

How heavy is this gift. We try to arrange our lives, we think we've found our voices. But in the background a melody is playing, which is familiar to us without our having ever been taught it. Everything gets mixed up. Interrupted lives blend with our own. We are beholden to those who were denied their right to a future, very beholden indeed. Their shadow falls over everything; their death requires that we issue a response. But how?

"I was put off by the insouciance of the middle-class society in which I lived," writes Helen Epstein of her childhood.

> I was scornful of my friends who could spend an entire day doing nothing. . . . In high school, where most of my friends dreamed of marrying well, or making a successful career, or having the money to buy fancy wardrobes, I dreamed of finding ways to suffer, to confront, feel and vanquish pain.
>
> . . . I felt that people who had never been victims were not altogether human.
>
> [. . . My parents] looked down on people who were complacent in their trouble-free lives.

Between the ages of thirteen and twenty, I forced my body to survive. I became sick; I fell prey to an insatiable hunger to be tested.

Anorexia is a monologue, which says that something is devouring us, that we are burning with the desire to live. Anorexia, I believe, is a promise of fidelity made to those who are absent. Anorexia is, I believe, the language spoken by those who inherit these silent stories.

We submit ourselves thoroughly to self-sacrifice, eager for the taste of suffering. We impose a crude daily discipline on ourselves, one of privation and exercise. We yield to nothing, not even our physiological necessities. We cherish hunger, emptiness; muscle pain and migraines are so many proofs of our valor.

We are on a crusade for excellence, for the exceptional, all the while knowing that we will never measure up to those who have preceded us, to their courage, their heroism, their grief, their devastation.

So we work away at being beyond saving. They will take us from one psychologist to another, as they try to figure out the source of this illness, as they proclaim that we refuse to be a woman, to grow up, to be alive. We will remain unspeaking. Because we won't be able to say that, on the contrary, by hovering so close to death, we are proclaiming our triumph over it.

* * *

"Why am I so profoundly convinced that these girls who let themselves die share a secret reason, that they seek to learn where life ends and death begins, because of something they ought to have been told, that they could not be told, something that makes them afraid," writes Geneviève Brisac in her novel *Petite.*

That "something" that the survivors could not tell—their children and grandchildren understand it.

Anorexia is the experience of absolute solitude, of vertigo. We can take refuge in the abyss, shut ourselves up in it. We can hurl ourselves against its walls, soundlessly, wordlessly.

Beside me in my solitude: writers, musicians, exiles, the stateless. I fed myself on their quests.

I have a particular affection for those who lay claim to no country, who glorify no land. Their deracinated writing takes root in the night, a night vaster than any landscape. They whirl from one identity to another; that's why I value them. We follow them as they wander and it's no bad thing to be lost, together.

I can decide to leave the Annex; I am not imprisoned here.

In my cowardice and naïveté, I thought I had the choice to be Jewish or not. From earliest childhood, I heard people saying anti-Semitic things. But they were not directed at me. The people who said them thought they were safe with me: they didn't think I was Jewish.

No doubt I bore little resemblance to their idea of a Jew. No doubt I was too blond, too pale; my father's surname, Lafon, gave them other ideas, and it provided a screen for my mother's foreign name.

"Jewish, you? But you don't seem like it at all," they said, intending it as a compliment, when I revealed my Jewishness. I didn't seem like it at all.

And sometimes I let them say it.

My grandparents worked so hard not to seem like it, as did my mother, like any other immigrants.

Work to make yourself invisible. Give your children names from the Christian calendar. Don't be conspicuous. Try to be a "good Jew" the way we talk about "good Muslims": go whole hog on a pâté au porc, celebrate Christmas, laugh at anti-Semitic jokes, or at the very least don't take offense. Don't talk about the Holocaust too much. *Move on.*

Otto Frank practiced a discreet Judaism, one that was inoffensive to the German bourgeoisie, of which he was a part. It was important to him to prove himself patriotic and exemplary; after the war, he did not break with this upbringing. His daughter may have been delighted, in her diary, at the assassination attempt on Hitler, on July 21, 1944; she may have written, in October 1942, that there is no greater hostility in the world than that between Germans and Jews; for his part, Otto Frank preferred to say, in 1969, that it was important not to "self-flagellate" for the sake of the past.

Otto Frank agreed to let screenwriters delete the passages in which his daughter wrote that she was terrified of the Nazis parading through Amsterdam, and others in which she described her attachment to Judaism. Perhaps a man who had survived Auschwitz could not bear to understand that his daughter *knew* what was in store for them. Maybe the survivor was still afraid. The past was so recent.

It is a sad irony that this fervent desire to assimilate should today be the very essence of conspiracy theories.

Someone who "doesn't seem" to be what they are is deeply suspect. At least a foreigner who doesn't disguise his difference admits he isn't one of us. Whereas someone who looks just like us . . . how are we to tell them apart? Isn't dissembling a red flag that they're up to something?

On January 11, 2015, I met up with some friends. We were stunned; it was impossible to talk about anything apart from the attacks. The editors of *Charlie Hebdo* and now the slaughter at the Hyper Cacher market.

Yes . . . but . . . it's not the *same,* a young woman said. She said, that day, that to murder men and women because they're Jews is *different* . . . without finishing her sentence.

That day, this young left-wing woman spoke like a right-wing man: Raymond Barre, who was the prime minister at the time of the attack on the rue Copernic on October 3, 1980. He said:

"This odious attack targeting Jews on their way to synagogue hit innocent French people, who were crossing the rue Copernic."

An old feminist slogan has it that a sexist on the right is no different from a sexist on the left. And so an anti-Semite on the right seems no different from an anti-Semite on the left: both think Jews are *not the same.* Still today, one in four French people thinks there is a "Jewish conspiracy."

The international appetite for television series about ultra-Orthodox Jews, from *Shtisel* to *Unorthodox,* is worth reflecting on. Maybe we like them because they are absolutely foreign to us, visibly distinct: fanatics who may be laughed at or mistrusted.

My grandparents spoke Russian, Polish, Hebrew, Yiddish, and French. They were secular Communists who didn't celebrate any of the Jewish holidays. They imagined themselves to be French.

Spellbound with pleasure, with the deference of guests, they made excuses for the country of the Rights of Man and cited Jaurès.

I remember how shocked they were after the attack on the rue des Rosiers. I am glad they died before they could learn about what happened to Ilan Halimi, the schoolchildren at Ozar Hatorah, and the men who went to do their shopping at the Hyper Cacher that day.

It must be dawn but you'd never know it in here; all the windows of the Annex are covered with opaque fabric, as they were in 1944.

In less than three hours, hundreds of people will line up to visit the Annex. In less than two hours, I will leave the museum, I will lose myself in this city, with no desire to find my way; I will walk for a long time, I will cry like children do, tears giving way to still more tears; a woman will approach me to ask if I'm alright and I will find myself incapable of responding. I will finally return to my hotel, drunk with fatigue; in vain I will look for the key to my room, dumping the contents of my bag on the marble floor of the reception area, before the impassive eyes of the young receptionist.

And to explain myself, I will stammer out these words: I spent the night at Anne Frank's house.

The dawn is tarnished by heavy rains, which strike the windows of the Annex. A summer rain, which calls you outside, a rain that breaks up the silence. It runs in rivulets down the transom window in the attic. The staircase leading up there is rigid, almost vertical. I lean on it, tilting my body to try to get a glimpse of the only room in the Annex where visitors are not allowed.

From this slanted position, you can see a tiny square of light, the only window, the sole aperture allowed in the Annex, opening to the sky.

From this slanted position, we can see what Anne Frank saw: "the blue sky, the bare chestnut tree glistening with dew . . . the dark, rainy evening, the wind, the racing clouds."

The landing was transformed into a bedroom for Peter, with whom Anne briefly fell in love.

She gave him pictures to decorate the walls of his room. When she offered him new ones, he turned them down: he looked at them every day, he said, and the people in them "have become my friends."

When they had had to leave their apartment and go into hiding, Peter's father also told him he could only take the essentials. The young man insisted on keeping his bicycle. Because one day, *afterward*, he would go for long rides along the Amstel, with or without Anne.

Peter found an ingenious place to keep his bicycle, in his semblance of a bedroom: he suspended it from the ceiling.

Peter van Pels died between April 11th and May 5th in 1945 in the camp of Mauthausen, a few days before it was liberated by the English.

I sat in the heart of this emptiness, faced with the heartbreaking optimism of a seventeen-year-old boy. Then, I walked around the Annex, and, once again, faced with the door to *her* room, I hesitated, retreated, and took the staircase leading back down to Otto Frank's office.

A few years after the *Diary* is published in the Netherlands, its devastated readers begin gathering outside the door of 263 Prinsengracht. They want to see *the* bedroom.

This sudden interest takes Otto Frank and the other employees of Opetka by surprise; the Annex is empty, no one sets foot in there, there's nothing to see. Only their offices and the warehouse where they keep spices and jams are accessible.

What is to be done with all these people, ever more numerous, who sometimes leave bouquets of flowers or little notes on the building's front stoop?

Otto Frank decides to allow some people into the Annex; all they have to do is make an appointment. Do these first visitors know that Anne's father is very close by in his office, that he can hear them whispering and crying?

Mr. Frank the survivor, who is accused by Holocaust deniers of having *invented* his daughter.

I've chosen not to mention them by name here: their identities are interchangeable. First they were former leaders of the Hitler Youth, then pamphleteers for the extreme right, conspiracy theorists, Holocaust deniers. They succeed one another, responding to each other, down the decades. They are obsessed by the subject, devoting many books and op-eds to it, and strewing comments across the internet about Anne Frank. But though I refuse to mention their names, I have to point out how dedicated they have been to erasing her. They find her unbearable: her writings are the proof we *knew*, they make it impossible to pretend that we didn't.

On October 9, 1942, Anne Frank writes: "Our many Jewish friends and acquaintances are being taken away in droves. The Gestapo is treating them very roughly and transporting them in cattle cars to Westerbork. . . . We assume that most of them are being murdered. The English radio says they're being gassed."

The Holocaust deniers work very hard but are somewhat lacking in rigor; for the most part it seems they haven't bothered to read the *Diary* in its entirety.

Impossible, says one, that the people hiding in the Annex would have been able to vacuum. Someone would have heard them. Anne Frank says they did housework when the building was empty, between noon and 1:00 p.m., or on Sundays.

But look! another crows triumphantly: these words were written with a ballpoint pen, which was extremely unusual in 1944! This "proof" is as misleading as the others. The bit of text written in ballpoint pen is composed on strips of paper inserted into the manuscript: the working notes of a graphologist who examined the authenticity of the diary in the 1960s. She confirmed it.

In 1959, when the play was being performed in Austria, a group of young neo-Nazis interrupted the performance and handed out a leaflet to the audience: "This story is a fraud. Anne Frank never existed. The Jews made her up to get more money. Don't believe a word of this, it's pure fiction."

That's when Simon Wiesenthal, the "Nazi hunter," decided to find the officer who arrested the Franks, to get him on the record: that would put an end to these attacks.

He found him in 1963. Silberbauer had since become an inspector in the criminal police force in Vienna; he had a clear memory of the Annex and his shock that eight people had managed to live there for two years. Silberbauer recognized Anne in a photograph he was shown, as well as Otto Frank. He remembered Otto Frank's German insignia, honoring his bravery in combat—"remarkable, for a Jew."

The investigation got Silberbauer temporarily suspended from his job. During the interrogation, he complained: he had just bought all new furniture that he hadn't finished paying off. If he couldn't work anymore, what was he going to do? He took offense; he was astonished at being questioned about this case, when he was only carrying out orders. Apart from that, he concluded, I have nothing else to say.

The Austrian judges decided there was nothing worth pursuing; the SS officers had done their job in arresting the Franks and sending them to Westerbork.

Silberbauer remained in his post.

These false claims that Anne Frank was a fraud have been contradicted by a number of historians, graphologists, and other specialists. But I know, we know, that it won't matter. It is the function of conspiracy theories to see any objection as proof of the conspiracy. No testimony, no expert witness will stop them from rewriting History.

Until his death Otto Frank fought against these attacks. He brought lawsuits; he agreed to let the *Diary* be examined by experts in 1959, 1961, and 1980. Miep Gies asserted under oath that she had witnessed Anne writing in her diary, the very same one she had kept hidden in a drawer.

The Institute of Forensic Medicine, the legal laboratory for the Dutch justice system, painstakingly reviewed the notebooks. They examined everything: the paper, the glue, the postcards stuck to the wall. They scrutinized every detail of Anne Frank's handwriting, and a graphologist, Dr. Mina Becker, even detected traces of physical decline due to a lack of physical activity and fresh air. A document that came in at 719 pages long confirmed the *Diary's* authenticity.

I can't help but wonder if, maybe, Anne Frank would have smiled at the idea that a hardened Holocaust denier offered as the ultimate proof of the *Diary*'s falsity that no fifteen-year-old girl would have been capable of thinking, much less writing, what he had read in it. It was way too inventive and irreverent for a girl.

The irreverence of teenage girls ought to receive much more attention than it does; it should be recorded and transmitted. We have to cherish those few short years when adolescent girls pay caution no heed and have yet to learn respect and remorse.

They lie fluidly and without hesitation, eat with their fingers, climb onto roofs, and, out walking arm in arm, they take up the entire sidewalk. The only thing they fear is ending up like us, running out of steam and complaining about the boundless energy of the young.

Parents like to tell stories about their babies' first words; they tear up thinking about how creative and funny their children are. But they regard the inevitable onset of adolescence like an approaching plague, like a meteor threatening civilization. How fearful we are of teenagers' extreme lucidity, their knowing gaze, which sees through all our concessions and compromises.

To reread our old journals is to confront ourselves with the people we used to be. Would our younger selves feel shame, or sadness, at seeing who we've become? Have we given up? Have we become too well-behaved, complacent, for lack of courage?

We all should reread our teenage diaries, to remain worthy of the challenge we once lay down.

What kind of adult would Anne Frank have become? Anne Frank, who swore "to achieve more than Mother ever did," who said she "goes into ecstasy" looking at the nude bodies of women, which got her censored by the fundamentalist Christians in America. She was a defiant young girl, who openly declared how seriously she took her writing, and whom Fritz Pfeffer called "self-centered" when she requested that they find an equitable way to share the small table in their room. "Him and his lies. I'll smack his ugly mug so hard he'll go bouncing off the wall!" she wrote after a dispute.

If there were a museum of irreverent young women, Anne Frank, who once described herself as "a frolicsome little goat tugging at its tether," would be its patron.

No doubt I am delirious from not sleeping, but around 5 a.m. I decide to make a list of everyone I'd like to see honored in this imaginary museum. I have been through the Annex several times already; there is nowhere else to go except the one room that refuses me entrance.

I sit on the linoleum in a corridor; I have no idea where it leads but I can at least recharge my computer here to spare the potential consequences of using a Second World War–era plug.

Since teenage defiance is more a state of mind than a reflection of how long we've been alive, we must make room in our imaginary museum for Laureen Nussbaum, age ninety-five.

During our first virtual meeting, Laureen's youthful energy rebuffed my ageist prejudice. When I asked her if Otto Frank had censored the pages of the diary in which Anne Frank reflects on her sexuality, she cut me off, booming "*NONSENSE.*"

Virginia Woolf would need a whole floor. We'd have to include Nina Simone as well. And I would also like to see my mother there, and all those who, like her, didn't know how irreverent they were, if only in secret, sometimes.

After beginning this list, my thoughts drift to the building that housed the museum. It would have to be unremarkable, so that its irreverence might strike us more boldly. A palace would crush it: its irreverence would be surrounded by too much arrogance.

Though the ostentation of some museums is a tribute to the splendor of the works they protect, others are more mischievous: they take up residence exactly where you'd least expect them.

In Bucharest, for example, the National Museum of Contemporary Art is located on the top floor of what was Ceaușescu's palace and which is, today, the home of Parliament.

This museum houses the work of artists born mostly after the fall of the Communist regime.

In 2010, I had the chance to see a painting that the museum had chosen not to display. I saw it with a friend who lived in the city, who asked if I wanted to see the hidden work.

After making sure that none of the museum staff were paying attention to us, my friend signaled for me to follow her discreetly. She knew the way by heart—she had already gone three times; she couldn't get enough of it.

At the end of a long hallway stood a banal-looking door. This was the place. The flashlight on her phone revealed a storeroom in complete disarray. They had stuck outdated furniture in here, along with dusty old rugs and an immense painting, which lay with its face against a wall.

It took us several attempts to move it. As if being left in a closet weren't sufficiently disgraceful, it was upside down as well. It took me a minute to recognize the features of Nicolae Ceaușescu. The painter had considerably improved and slimmed him; he looked healthy, his hair shining and his waist cinched in a gray suit. He was surrounded by a dozen or so Pioneers with rosy cheeks, beaming at him.

No doubt the painter received much acclaim for his painting in 1988, and maybe he was even proud of it. But surely today he would prefer to forget his contribution to a dictatorship.

We stayed there for a long while, in that closet, in the heart of defunct Communism.

We swapped childhood memories. The ex-president was part of them. We chuckled at the vanity common to all heads of state, who, today, require that pictures of them be photoshopped to camouflage their love handles, their wrinkles, their small stature.

In the museum's guest book, we left a short note: this painting was in ridiculously bad taste, but what was even worse was the idea that hiding it would erase years of collaboration from our memories.

But perhaps I'm the one who was in bad taste, that day, in taking more of an interest in what was hidden away in a storeroom than what was hung on the museum's walls.

I am fascinated by people who are said to have good taste. Spending time with them brings out a childish inferiority complex. I admire their way of looking chic while wearing *nothing special* and the sober decor in their apartment. Next to them I feel vulgar and badly dressed.

Taste is not innate; it is an unforgiving social marker of the context in which we were raised, the education we were allowed to attain. Good taste—know-how—is something we inherit, along with the confidence that comes with that kind of knowledge.

People say that the Impressionist painters are "populist" because they are "easy to access"; an acclaimed film is too "mainstream"; we talk about "people" without ever counting ourselves among them.

While I was writing *The Little Communist Who Never Smiled,* I remember reading a number of articles excoriating Nadia Comăneci's "bad taste" when she arrived in the United States in 1989, having defected from Romania.

Rather than writing about the gymnast's performances, people dissected her appearance: her "loud" blue eyeshadow, her "cheap" blond hair, her "frumpy" fake leather jacket—all of this "typical" for Eastern Europe.

A few years ago, during a European residency, I was asked to show a pair of Scandinavian artists around Bucharest. They had no interest in the splendor of its Orthodox churches, or its Art Nouveau buildings, or the improvised performances given by poets in abandoned Victorian houses. They were after something else: instances of what they referred to as "kitsch." They took pictures of themselves in front of a boutique, pointing to an old-fashioned synthetic flowered housecleaner's blouse. They openly made fun of a café waitress's very high heels and looked doubtful when I praised the vitality of the local rap scene.

These artists were recently the subject of an article in a magazine about interior design; the reporter commented on their "knowing taste." I remember the brutality of this taste, their certainty in being its custodians.

My own taste is disorganized. It has no notion of hierarchies; it runs from the glitter and sparkle of musical theatre to Bartók's Romanian dances, from transcendent pages in the writing of Paul Nizan to those of authors who are considered second-rate, whose novels, in my teenage years, greatly moved me.

No doubt my family bequeathed me their bad taste: my grandparents' home was a jumble of useless objects, worthless, with no aesthetic value: souvenirs from countries fled in haste. I also inherited a certain unease, a feeling of discomfort in the places where good taste is decided.

When I was offered the chance to spend a night in the museum of my choice, at no point did I picture myself in an art museum. I take great pleasure in visiting them, but I don't feel authorized to give my opinion on what is shown there.

Daring to open the door to a museum implies that we are not afraid of losing ourselves inside. It is the territory of those who know how to navigate it; the others admire the setting, guests who are careful not to knock anything over, who will read all the captions and listen to all the explanations provided by the audio guide.

The regulars will carry on conversations as if they were in a café; others will whisper, as if in a place of worship.

My grandmother spoke three languages: Polish, Yiddish, and French. She was a survivor who knew how to conjugate the word *fight* in the imperative; she was conscientious about the fact that fighting was necessary, would again be necessary if for some reason all of *that* started up again.

But whenever she described a radio program devoted to a writer or a director, her voice changed. It was the spellbound voice of someone who had once been a young girl in Lublin, full of dreams and longings, but who was unable to do anything, have anything.

My grandmother stood outside the doorway to culture, hungry for it, deprived of it. It intimidated her. She could only access art when it was described by others. How she loved and was devoted to them: Bernard Pivot, Jacques Chancel, Ève Ruggieri. She called them by their first names, repeated what they said.

Ida was born in Poland around 1914, in Lublin, a city that was nicknamed the Jewish Oxford, where culture thrived: theatre, literature, theology, science.

The premature death of her father, a teacher, threw her family of previously modest means into poverty. When she was eight years old, she had to leave school and go out to work; she cleaned houses for rich Polish people. In the evening, local volunteers (members of the Bund, a movement of socialist, secular Jews) taught her some basic history and mathematics, as well as reading and writing.

Her older brother had left for France in 1925 at the age of fifteen, disgusted by the daily anti-Semitism he faced in Poland. He told his sister many times: there was no future for them there.

He sent her a postcard with these words written on it: *Come to Paris.*

1930. Ida doesn't have time to learn French, but it doesn't matter: what is required of her, in the Parisian hair salon where she manicures nails, is that she work dexterously and smile.

The young man she meets at the Russian immigrants' dance has a first name for every country he's lived in: he was born Grichka in Russia, renamed Herschel and then Zwi when he moved to Palestine. In France he would become Georges the bellboy, the taxi driver, the handyman, the peddler of secondhand Bibles, and even the orderly for Maréchal Juin.

They marry, each dreaming of being naturalized; one day they would be ordinary French people. But the fiction of a France of *liberty, equality, fraternity* was short-lived: the law concerning the status and exclusion of Jews was enacted on October 3, 1940.

Ida taught her daughter—my mother—to keep quiet before she could even speak. Not to give her real name, with its foreign consonants. Ida and Georges hid their daughter in barns and in convents, as well as with the Protestant families who opened their homes to them, from the villages of Vif en Isère to Chambon-sur-Lignon in the Haute-Loire.

1945. They survived. Ida and Georges can finally return home to Paris. The locks to their apartment have been changed, and some strangers have taken up residence. All their belongings—their furniture, their dishes—have been divided up among the neighbors. The rest was thrown away: official papers, letters from brothers and sisters who stayed behind in Poland and Russia, family photos. We thought you weren't coming back, the concierge said, by way of explanation. Nothing is left of their past. Ida is in her thirties, with two children. She has recurrent nightmares, which her sleeping pills wipe away. Tuberculosis as well. And a devastated husband: his parents and sisters have died in Auschwitz-Birkenau.

As for Ida's two elder sisters, they died of hunger, imprisoned in the Polish ghetto.

Ida didn't have the time to learn to read or write French until she was well over the age of sixty.

The postcards she sent me were signed with her name, but written by my grandfather. She was ashamed for me to see her awkward, childish handwriting.

But even if she couldn't write, she understood everything about literature.

It was a stage set library that first invited her in: the television program *Apostrophes.* Bernard Pivot reigned over my grandmother's Friday nights. He put an end to every telephone conversation: I'm hanging up, it's time for *Apostrophes.*

She was amazed: they came to her, Nabokov and Kundera, she was actually meeting them, Duras and Truffaut. The France of *Apostrophes* compensated for that of the neighbors, who pronounced her surname suspiciously.

Ida only found respite in fiction, in the novels she slowly began to decipher when she was more than seventy years old.

It was because of her, Ida Goldman, that I was spending the night in the Annex. She was the one who gave me—I must have been around ten—a golden medallion stamped with the portrait of Anne Frank. The portrait was awkward and looked more like a forty-year-old woman—offering Anne Frank the future she didn't get to have. You must always keep this medallion, explained my grandmother. *Never forget.*

* * *

Some worthless objects are, to us, infinitely precious. They remind us of a person, of a love, of a place that no longer exists. We can't bear the idea of losing them, but we have trouble looking at them, so great is their evocative power. We keep them hidden away, in a box, an envelope, in the margins of memory.

Until my night in the Annex, these "things" to which I am so attached seemed to have nothing in common, except my fear of losing them.

My Anne Frank medallion, a blue plastic rosary, a dozen letters written on thin, translucent paper. And the photo booth picture of the boy who sent them to me. A boy wearing a cable-knit sweater, his hair carefully smoothed back for the photograph.

The night brought them together.

The night is over. It's 5:34 a.m.; I've been sleeping for an hour. When I awake, for a few moments, the emptiness of the Annex confuses me; I don't recognize anything but I am brought back to the present by Margot Frank, gazing at me from a framed photograph.

Margot makes me think of those friends from adolescence in whom we confided everything, later realizing we hadn't learned much about them at all. The kind of girl who excelled in all subjects but whom we couldn't manage to resent—she did it all with such ease. The kind of girl whose ironic sense of humor emerged precisely at the moment when we were starting to find her overly serious.

On May 16, 1944, Anne made an admiring list of all the things her big sister was studying in hiding: English, French, Latin, geometry, physics, chemistry, algebra, English literature, French literature, German literature, Dutch literature, accounting, geography and history, biology, and economics. She was also taking classes in stenography and was interested in mechanics. What did she like to read? Whatever came her way, with a preference for anything to do with religion and medicine.

Margot was also very athletic; she rowed on the Amstel. In the summer of 1941, the trainer Roos van Gelder took a photograph of her team. Dressed in white shorts and blouses, they attempt to look at the camera, blinded by the sun. You can make out the remnants of a picnic on the grass; a young girl is voraciously licking her plate clean while Margot, to her right, breaks out in laughter, her face turned to the sky. A few weeks later, a new law will force her to leave the team as well as her high school to attend an establishment reserved for Jews.

Margot, the place where the story begins, for whom the Franks went into hiding earlier than planned. Margot the mystery, whose journal has never been found, the lost pages of an interrupted life.

Pages that, perhaps, someone in Amsterdam kept. Perhaps someone has read them. And perhaps this someone has a reason for not sharing them with us, for keeping Margot tucked away in the past, safe from people's interpretations, analyses, and obsessions. Margot Frank, who silently began to cry when the Nazis invaded the Annex. Margot, the big sister, whose father said that he would never forget the way she looked at him when they were separated at Auschwitz.

Margot, who dreamed of becoming a nurse or a midwife in Palestine, after the war.

In drawing, a vanishing point is "an imaginary point intended to help the artist give a sense of perspective in his picture." Margot, who vanished from history, is my point of reference in the museum. She is the one who points the way.

Her gaze follows me, asking me: So?

In an hour, I will leave. Surely I can't be on my way, just like that? Without having taken the time to say hello to her kid sister?

The church bells chime and I have to stop pacing, fleeing. It is six o'clock in the morning. I am so late that the hour no longer matters.

The surveillance cameras can't measure our cardiac rhythms; no doubt I appear perfectly serene as I push open the door to Anne Frank's room.

I murmur her name, awkward and embarrassed: I still don't know what to call her—Anne Frank, Anne. The real pictures, on the wall, are yellowed; some are torn. They are layered on top of one another, canceling each other out, according to the young girl's changing affections. A pop culture mosaic that doesn't give a hoot about good taste: chimpanzees around a table elbow to elbow with little girls with excessively blond hair; Michelangelo's *Pietà* covering up a picture of a collaborationist figure skater; Michelangelo and Hollywood deferring to a laughing princess barely twelve years old: Elizabeth of York.

I think of other princesses, bodies made of sweat and pain, feigning lightness, made entirely of tulle and satin: Princess Aurora and the Sylphs; the white or black swans of the great classic ballets. Dancers are messengers of the ineffable; they carry the extinguished grace of an old, forgotten star. The dance is transmitted gesture by gesture, from one dancer to another, the slightest inflection of a wrist is whispered, like a secret.

What should we have done with what we've inherited? How to follow these traces without effacing them?

The emptiness at the beginning of the night has become a brief quietude, a parenthesis. I am at the edge of the abyss, but I am no longer afraid.

I sit down on the ground in *that* room. I open my notebook and, without thinking about it, I write down a last name and a first name. Two syllables. Into the vacant room of a young girl whose name is famous all over the world slips the shadow of a young man you've never heard of. He will always be fifteen years old. He is posing in the photo booth picture I keep tucked away with my Anne Frank medallion.

A few days before I went to Amsterdam, for no particular reason, I bought a book called *The Missing Picture* (2015) by Rithy Panh and Christophe Bataille. In my notebook, I copied out the following quote:

> For many years, I have been looking for a missing picture: a photograph taken between 1975 and 1979 by the Khmer Rouge, when they ruled over Cambodia. On its own, of course, a photograph does not prove mass murder; but it prompts us to think, to meditate, to build history.
>
> I searched for it in vain in the archives, in old papers, in the villages of my country. Now I know: this picture must be missing.
>
> . . . Some images must be missing always, always being replaced by others. In this movement there is life, struggle, difficulty and beauty, the sadness of faces lost, the comprehension of what was once: sometimes nobility, and even courage: never oblivion. . . . And now I give this missing picture to you, so it will never stop looking for you.

The young man in the cable-knit sweater is a missing picture and I give it to you. I never talk about him because it is impossible to talk about his life without lamenting his death. I have never written his name anywhere but my diary. He appears in no novel because I refuse to disguise him as a character; reality owes him an infinite debt, life has to create a place for him.

Here, perhaps, in this room, the young man's name can be spoken.

Of his life I can give only a short account, mainly of the dozen or so days we spent together. These words, *spent together*, refer to the moments we shared, between living people. We don't count the time spent with the dead, time spent *being* together, tangibly, with the help of memory, things that remind us of them, letters exchanged.

As for the end of his story—I can guess it, I know it, though for decades I have avoided imagining it.

In 1976, the young man is fifteen years old, a boarder at a Parisian high school. His parents live in Bucharest; his father works at the Cambodian embassy.

One day in March, the father receives an official document relieving him of his duties and ordering him to return to Phnom Penh.

The father is one of the last representatives of the former regime still in his post; it's been months since the others returned to the country, since Pol Pot and the Khmer Rouge took power on April 17, 1975.

The father calls his son and tells him to come to Bucharest as quickly as he can. From there, they will return to their country together, as a family.

The young man is meant to stay in Bucharest for a week and a half or so, a period of transition between his Parisian high school and whatever awaits them in Cambodia.

While his parents organize the move, the young man isn't sure how to occupy himself in this city where he knows no one.

His little brother is placed in his care; they are told to go spend some time in the Cișmigiu Gardens.

This park, the oldest in the city, is protected from the Communist aesthetic. Wooden bridges connect artificial islands littered with water lilies; a bandstand and guinguettes recall the Buttes-Chaumont.

The young man is sitting on a bench and reading, without paying too much attention to his brother, who is playing with some kids his age—three little girls, between the ages of eight and ten.

The redhead is Dutch; her parents work at the embassy. The other, the oldest of the group, is Romanian; she lives alone with her mother in the suburbs. I am the blond one, the youngest of the three; I live not far from the park.

The brother, who is in my class at school, proudly introduces us to his older brother: he lives in Paris! And later on he'll be a diplomat, like our father. Certainly not, the young man retorts, irritated; he won't be a diplomat or a soldier, contrary to their mother's wishes. Later on he'll read novels and listen to music all day, that's what he'll do.

No doubt he is a bit bored that first afternoon, watching us play hopscotch on the asphalt, listening to our schoolkids' stories.

If he comes back the next day, it's likely because he has nowhere else to go.

We, however, are surprised and delighted to have someone who is almost a grown-up to talk to, a high school student, the kind who normally wouldn't give us a second glance.

That day, he won't have the time to read even a single page. We want to know everything about Paris: about his dorm, his friends, the records he listens to—his world is foreign three times over, since he is a boy, a teenager, and lives in the West.

We bring him into our secret world.

Over there, those ruins, are an old monastery; they say there's a hidden underground passageway but we've never dared go exploring. In winter, we go ice-skating on the lake, here, and later on, we're holding a roller-skating race on this circular track, the Rotonda *scriitorilor,* the writers' rotunda. The twelve statues depict famous authors.

Since he seems to like reading so much, does he know Mihai Eminescu? We learned one of his poems at school last week:

A tomorrow is added to your days,
A yesterday is taken from your life,
Yet before you,
It is only today that stands.

We pepper him with questions: how is he going to make up his classwork if he doesn't go to school anymore? And why does he have to go back to Cambodia?

Today, I have only a vague memory of what he told us. Eight-year-olds aren't very interested in politics. I remember he explained how diplomatic service worked; his parents were allowed to stay in Bucharest after the regime change because his father was an ambassador.

As for the rest, the young man has only a vague notion of what was going on in Cambodia; he knows the name of the prime minister, he is a Communist, that's about it.

Maybe his ignorance was real: he was in Paris when the Khmer Rouge invaded Phnom Penh in April 1975. If he read the newspapers, he would have seen them extol the "obvious popular enthusiasm" of the inhabitants of Phnom Penh, noting positively that "not a drop of blood was spilled."

But maybe, in the spring of 1976, the young man already suspects that the Western narrative is a horrifying rewriting of reality. That day, he tells us nothing.

We hardly know him but already he's all we can talk about at recreation. We gush over his style, which is so Parisian; he wears jeans and Fruit of the Loom t-shirts, which are impossible to find in Bucharest. And apart from that, what's so special about him? our classmates ask. He listens to us. He asks us questions. And if he gets our names confused, he apologizes.

We agree to meet at the park after school, in the same place where we first met him. When he finally appears, we run toward him. He puts his fingers in his ears, exaggeratedly—how can such little people make such a big noise—but he came back, without his little brother, just for us.

But on this second day, he seems preoccupied; he misses his friends from school. His slightly weary sadness moves us, at the same time as it delights us, because it offers us a challenge: to distract him and cheer him up.

We can't just let him sit there on his bench. We declare him the referee of our jump rope game. We make up new rules. He smiles, even laughs at the way we boast and fall over when we attempt a backward somersault to impress him.

He laughs at our television references, which are so out of date—in France, no one watches *Bewitched* anymore! And when he asks us to teach him some polite expressions in Romanian, we teach him our favorite insults.

That evening at dinner, I mention him for the first time.

Why is a fifteen-year-old boy hanging out with little girls? My parents' barely disguised suspicion infuriates me. They insist on thinking logically; so much love for someone who's basically a stranger makes no sense to them.

Is it love? Of course not. Love is so small, it makes you jealous and anxious, but none of us is trying to possess him. We share him, he brings us together, he unites us, like a refrain.

Children have all the time in the world, so they make good use of it by forgetting it. Time doesn't exist; it defers to the years that divide us. We are in a hurry to grow up, while the young man is momentarily escaping his adult-adjacent life to become a kid again.

He returns to the park the following day, as well as the day after.

He's a kid, now, snorting at our jokes, slurping down vanilla ice cream for lunch, falling over trying to do handstands on the grass, losing his glasses several times a day, decreeing that my dog must be trained and then immediately changing his mind and covering him with kisses. Just a kid, who begs to play Red Light Green Light 123 one more time when we're tired of it, a bad loser who cheats at cards, but also a kid who's got a lot on his mind, who's soon going to have to go through his things, all the stuff he's brought from Paris, clothes, records, books. His parents are encouraging him to get to it; they can't take too much with them when they go. Just the essential. They'll come back for the rest later, once their lives are set up in Phnom Penh.

How is he to know what's essential, he sighs. He asks each of us in turn: what would you bring?

Delighted with this new game and flattered to be asked a question, I make an inventory of my belongings: I wouldn't go anywhere without my stuffed monkey, my leotard, my *Fantômette* collection, my dog, and especially my diary.

Is he just pretending not to know that none of this is a game?

The springtime is morning blue, the winter is fading away in the acid sweetness of the freesias. We had almost forgotten time; ten days have slipped by.

Tomorrow, the young man will leave Bucharest.

Our last afternoon we can't stop laughing, our sadness disguised as hilarity. We offer him a bouquet of flowers picked from the park. We recite a poem we've written for him; we sing a song we've been practicing; I dance a bit of the *Nutcracker,* barefoot on the gravel, to the surprise of the other people walking through the park.

We want him to promise he'll come back in June to come to the end-of-the-year show at school. We want him to promise he'll be there in July, so we can all go to the beach together in Constanța.

He makes fun of us, grumbling that we sing off-key, that I dance badly, that we have no talent, what does he care about a bunch of kids putting on a show. Then, with tears in his eyes, he suddenly stands up. We have to say goodbye, right now; he hates drawn-out farewells.

He leaves.

We miss him. His sudden departure elicits in us the difficult feeling that in Romanian we call *dor,* a bittersweet blend of nostalgia, melancholy, and joy—the joy of having loved.

One morning, the oldest one of the group breaks down in tears at recreation; her parents told her *some things* about Cambodia. She whispers something that I later write down in my diary: we will remember meeting this boy all our lives.

On April 25th, after I've gone back to school, I find an envelope in the mailbox: the young man has written to me.

I have never received any mail, except for postcards from my grandparents. I wait until I'm alone in my bedroom to read his letter. It was sent from Moscow, where his family stopped off for a few days. The young man's parents had worked there, before being assigned to Bucharest.

I discover his way of interrupting his sentences with parentheses, which he sometimes forgets to close; I discover the music of his silent words, that he prefers to write.

He tells me in great detail about their journey, which promises to be quite a long haul. First the train from Bucharest to Moscow to Beijing, and then an airplane to Phnom Penh.

The sleeping berths on the train are very uncomfortable; his parents are in a bad mood; the lack of privacy is getting to him; he and his brothers fight incessantly. He is lonely, too. Moscow is boring. He has to go see all his parents' friends to say goodbye, attend endless dinners with grown-ups. Writing to us helps him; it's a bit like talking to us. He would so like to hear from us, but he doesn't yet have a fixed address.

He asks me to forgive his bad mood the day he left. He was very upset to have to leave us.

The postscripts pile up: oh and also, how is my dog? And also, did I finally understand the math problem he explained to me?

And also, we were like little sisters to him.

In my diary, I write him entire pages; later on, I will send them to him.

Writing is an obstinately hopeful gesture, proof of a senseless optimism. The young man writes to me though his daily life is just a series of dull hours spent on a train; he has nothing much to tell me.

He decides to look toward another horizon—he seizes hold of time, bends it to his will; he projects me into the future, amusing himself by imagining me as a young woman. My life to come unfolds on sheet after sheet of thin paper, a delicate shade of blue, given him by someone who works on the Soviet train since all the pages of his notebook are full.

When you grow up . . .

Maybe you'll be a lawyer? That would suit you, since you're so bad at losing.

Maybe you'll be a detective or a journalist, since you're always writing things down in your notebook.

While my future is worthy of entire pages, his own warrants only occasional, oblique references. His future is conditional. *My first life is over,* he writes. *If I only knew what the next would be like.*

He so loved being a student, especially French class. By the way, as an homage to the esteemed poets of Cișmigiu Park, here are some lines he studied; sorry this is all he can remember, apologies to Apollinaire:

Love goes away the way this water flows
  Love goes away
How slowly life goes
And how violently alive is hope.

He writes to us. We read each other our letters.

He writes to me. And he has so much to say that he writes right up to the edge of the paper; he scribbles sideways, in circles, his words lean forward, they go galloping with memories: we had a good time in the park, didn't we, with our stupid games. Some sentences squish together at the bottom of the page, elbowing each other for room: *I feel so torn, I feel like I'm getting farther away from you, my last link to the first part of my life. Everything is going to change completely. I know it. I would give anything to . . .*

He reconsiders, crossing out what comes next so many times it becomes illegible.

We try to decipher what he has decided not to share with us. Something seeps through, saturating the young man's sentences with a new heaviness.

I read the letter to my parents; they don't say anything. Maybe they don't know, yet. Or maybe they decide it's impossible to explain Pol Pot's "policy." Perhaps they've seen in the newspaper the list of the people who belong to an "impossible to re-educate underclass" who are being systematically murdered.

Journalists, doctors, lawyers, Buddhists, Muslims, Chams, Christians, intellectuals, teachers, managers, diplomats. Students. People who speak a foreign language. And people who wear glasses.

His last letter was sent from Beijing, dated May 4th.

The family had stopped there for a week, before flying to Phnom Penh. He's no longer a kid; he's transformed into an adult with somber foresight. *Tomorrow is my birthday; we won't celebrate it, it's no big deal, now is no time for fun. We won't be in touch for a long time; I think it will be a while before I can send letters from my country.*

So to make up for his silence, as a sign of friendship, he offers me this, slipped into the envelope: his light blue rosary, with plastic beads. *You know what this means to me. May you believe in what you want, may you believe.*

The other night, he said, he had listened to his favorite records, the ones he bought in Paris. His parents worried they'd have to pay extra to pack them in their luggage; in the end he had to leave them in Beijing.

So he gave himself a magnificent concert, bringing Blondie, Jacques Higelin, and the Bee Gees together on the same stage.

One song, in particular, he played over and over.

It's pretty old but it doesn't age. It really moves me, I don't know why. The more I listen to it, the more its meaning escapes me, even if I listened to it for years. Or maybe it's better not to try to understand it, or explain it.

I started a joke
Which started the whole world crying

. . . .

Till I finally died, which started the whole world living
Oh, if I'd only seen that the joke was on me

The final words of his final letter were like a veiled prayer, a goodbye that only pretended to be casual.

Let's make a pact, if that's ok: when you listen to this song, you'll think of me.

P.S. Don't forget me too quickly, now.

P.P.S. I'm asking you not to forget me too quickly.

When I listen to this song, I will think of you, Charles Chea. But I won't be able to listen to this song without thinking of you, so I don't listen to this song.

P.S. In the video for "I Started a Joke," black question marks float in slow motion, drawn around the musicians.

P.P.S. I became a writer.

Charles Chea was fifteen years old, he was a high school student, he spoke three languages, he wore glasses, his parents were diplomats, his mother was Christian.

For the Khmer Rouge, Charles Chea was just a stain to wipe away, a cancer to eradicate, a teenager to slaughter.

He opened the door to Anne Frank's house for me. May he keep her company, across the years that separate them.

How to end a story without bringing it to a close? Perhaps by leaving it full of silences, as in music: a breath between two notes, the promise there will be a next one.

The people we've lost haven't disappeared; they are here. They remain, and the trace of their absence is a question.

What can be done with one single night: it would take years to reply. There is so little time, there is never enough. There will never be enough time for the living to respond to the dead.

May their absence seek us out, may it never stop seeking us out.

I left the bedroom with its pictures on the walls. There were too many voices echoing inside. There were too many people around her, and also never enough. Anne Frank belonged not to her father, nor to the film producers, nor even to the historians, and certainly not to me. I knew we had to stop claiming ownership over her, even though, especially though, we all just want to take her in our arms.

I left the walkie-talkie on the camp bed. I said goodbye to Margot. The floors in the contemporary museum were damp and smelled like synthetic lilac. A man in a blue uniform was waiting for me at reception; he held out a rectangular package, a gift from the museum.

I protected it from the rain for a little while, and then I unwrapped it in the middle of the street. It was a framed black and white photograph of the attic window. The one through which you could see, if you leaned over, a scrap of sky, a single glint of light, escaping.

Thank you, Ronald Leopold, Saskia Matheron, and Teresien da Silva, and thanks as well to Gladys Herman, from the Anne Frank House.

Thank you, Margot Djikgraaf, for your shawl.

Thank you, Laureen Nussbaum, who was essential to this project.

Thank you, Rosetta Musaph-Andriesse, who goes by "Ted," for the tea, the company, and your words.

Thank you, Florence Illouz and Marc Semo, through whom I met Henriette Asséo and Annette Wieviorka: all four recommended works that were invaluable.

This book also owes much to *L'Intégrale Anne Frank* (Calmann-Lévy) [*The Collected Works of Anne Frank*, Bloomsbury], which brings together all her writings as well as essays by Mirjam Pressler, Gerhard Hirschfeld, and Francine Prose; also *Anne Frank Unbound* by Barbara Kirshenblatt-Gimblett and Jeffrey Shandler (Indiana University Press).

Thank you, Jeanne Bloch, who introduced me to Anat Meruk, who introduced me to David Wertheim of the Institute for Jewish Cultural and Social Studies in Amsterdam.

Thank you, Burint Saray, for taking the time and the trouble to listen to the story of Charles Chea and to speak with me.

Thank you, Alina Gurdiel, for your faith in this story, and thanks as well to Manuel Carcassonne and Paloma Grossi.

Thank you, Marie-Catherine Vacher, always.

Thank you, Isabelle Lafon, for being there.

Thank you to my first reader, Luis Pitiot.

I can't thank you enough, Olivier Lambert, for all these galaxies; the story goes on.

For Jeanne, maman.

TRANSLATOR'S NOTE

Some of the sources quoted in this book are taken from the following translations:

Guillaume Apollinaire, "The Pont Mirabeau," in *Zone: Selected Poems,* trans. Ron Padgett (New York: NYRB Classics, 2015).

Denis Diderot, *Jacques the Fatalist and His Master,* trans. J. Robert Loy (New York: Norton, 1978).

Mihai Eminescu, "With Life's Tomorrow Time You Grasp," trans. Alina Popescu (unpublished manuscript).

Anne Frank, *The Diary of a Young Girl: The Definitive Edition,* trans. Susan Massotty (London: Penguin, 1997).

Miep Gies and Alison Leslie Gold, *Anne Frank Remembered* (New York: Simon & Schuster, 1992).

Pierre Goldman, *Dim Memories of a Polish Jew Born in France*, trans. Joan Pinkham (New York: Viking, 1977).

Marlen Haushofer, *The Wall,* trans. Shaun Whiteside (Minneapolis, MN: Cleis Press, 1990).

Roberto Juarroz, "Vertical Poetry—Excerpts," trans. W. S. Merwin, in *Winter Springs* 19 (Winter 1987).

Georges Perec, *Ellis Island,* trans. Harry Mathews (New York: New Directions, 2021).

Elie Wiesel, *Day,* trans. Anne Borchardt (New York: Hill and Wang, 2006, originally published in English in 1962 as *The Accident*).

All other translations are my own.